C0046 35207

D1649438

N;
Ph

This l
renev
date

Praise for *The Slippery Year*

'Gideon explores her pain, doubt, regret, and confusion ... with great poise and insight and, ultimately, a gentle aura of hope' *Elle*

'There is nothing contrived, trite, or holier-than-thou in this crisply hilarious, candid, and affecting contemplation' *Booklist*

'Refreshing and sassy, with more than a dash of tenderness thrown in' *Kirkus Reviews*

'By the end of the book I felt like I had just spent several hours knocking back drinks with an especially funny friend'
The New Yorker

'Gideon is a good enough writer to make even some male readers ... understand ... at least a little bit about what women want'
The Daily Beast

'This self-deprecating, wickedly funny and mildly philosophical reflection on marriage, mothering, middle age and the march toward life's meaning will ring true for midlife women' *Bookpage*

'Gideon doesn't need to detonate her life to shake things up – there's a perfect storm raging inside her head, and its hilarity is drama enough for anyone' *San Francisco Magazine*

'Obliquely insightful and quirkily witty, with moments of touching tenderness to be found amid Gideon's tough talk'
The Barnes and Noble Review

The Slippery Year

The Slippery Year

How One Woman Found Happiness In Everyday Life

MELANIE GIDEON

Weidenfeld & Nicolson
LONDON

First published in Great Britain in 2010 by
Weidenfeld & Nicolson
an imprint of the Orion Publishing Group Ltd
Orion House, 5 Upper St Martin's Lane,
London WC2H 9EA
An Hachette Livre UK Company

1 3 5 7 9 10 8 6 4 2

A CIP catalogue record for this book is available
from the British Library.

ISBN: 978 0 297 86057 0

Printed in Great Britain by CPI Mackays, Chatham ME5 8TD

The Orion Publishing Group's policy is to use papers that are
natural, renewable and recyclable and made from wood grown in sustainable
forests. The logging and manufacturing processes are expected to conform
to the environmental regulations of the country of origin.

Every effort has been made to fulfil requirements with regard to
reproducing copyright material. The author and publisher will
be gla

For BHR and BGR

Author's Note

Some names have been changed to protect identities. In a few instances timelines and events have been compressed.

Introduction

One day when I was sitting in the carpool line waiting to pick my son up from school, it occurred to me that I had been sleepwalking through my life. This realization wasn't precipitated by some traumatic event. I did not have cancer. My parents had not abused me. I was in a good marriage to a kind man. But something wasn't right. I felt empty—an unrelenting, existential kind of emptiness. By all markers I was living a happy enough existence, but somehow I wasn't feeling it.

I had the sense that darker times were coming—any fool knows an abundance of light casts a long shadow. Still, right now I was well. I knew exactly how my afternoon would unfold. In a few minutes I would spy my son walking down the street swinging his backpack. We would stop at the market on our way home and buy a chicken to roast for dinner and some cream for our morning coffee—all those simple pleasures awaited me. It was a perfectly lovely moment. Why then, wasn't I inside of it? How had I slipped away? And most important, could I pull myself back?

The Slippery Year is the story of how I come to terms with my *happily ever after.* It's a conversation—personal and universal, funny and heartrending—about all the things that matter: children, the Sunday paper, sisters, good-hair days, dogs, love, loss, the passage of time, and all the reasons to go on living even when the only thing we can be sure of is that one day it will all end.

So who am I? I am a woman who forgot Julia Child came to my house for dinner (she came to my engagement party, too—I forgot that as well). I am a woman who is discovering the advantages of invisibility (I finally have a superpower), a woman who wants to fall in love with her husband all over again (if only he would stop buying vans on the Internet). I am one of the millions who is currently walking around in a daze, no longer recognizing herself, wondering *Is this all there is?*

This is the story of my slippery year.

The Slippery Year

September

WHENEVER MY HUSBAND CASUALLY SAYS, "HEY, HON, COME TAKE A LOOK at this Web site," I know it's going to cost me. All of our largest purchases have been preceded by my being summoned to his computer in this manner. So when he says this a few weeks before his birthday, I knew it's really going to cost me, and I don't mean just financially.

"Check this out," he says, pointing. "Isn't it cool?"

I glance at the Ford E-350 on his screen. It looks like the sort of vehicle that shuttles retirees to the local mall. "Kind of," I reply.

He frowns and says, "It's not just any old van. It's a camper. It would be perfect for us. You said you wanted to see the West."

I do want to see the West, in theory anyway. In fact, seeing the West was one of the reasons we moved with our nine-year-old son, Ben, to California. But travel takes so much planning, and as

I've gotten older I'm increasingly less willing to tolerate discomfort: the crowds, the traffic, everybody trying to reach the same place at the same time.

His fingers pound at the keyboard. "It's got captain's seats."

"What's a captain's seat?"

"That means it's very, very comfortable."

"Nice," I say, getting back to my book.

Ten minutes later, he says, "I'm going to get one for us."

"Us?" I say.

"Yes, us—you know, you and me?"

The subtext being: Aren't you lucky you married a man who wants to buy a family van as his midlife-crisis vehicle instead of a Porsche Carrera GT?

The good news is he finds a used van. The bad news is it's in South Dakota. So he pays somebody to fly to South Dakota, pick up the van and drive it back.

"It's an amazing deal," he says. "It only has fifteen thousand miles on it, and the woman is a motivated seller."

Once the van is on its way, my husband tells me the truth. The woman was not the original owner; her son was, or had been. He bought the van to go kayaking in the most untouched places. Then one day he went out in his boat and never returned. This van delivered him to his death. And now his heartbroken mother had sold it to us.

"You have to give it back," I tell him. "He died in it."

"He didn't die in it. He died in his kayak."

"Well, he might as well have died in the van," I say. "He was in the van right before he died."

My husband sighs.

I want him to be happy, us to be happy. It seems every day

we hear that another couple has decided to call it quits. More often than not in our circle, the wife leaves the husband. When talking divorce with these women—mothers, like me, of school-age children—we speak in a shorthand that ricochets around in my head like the rhymes of Dr. Seuss.

They say: Feeling dead. Dead in bed. Too much snore. There's got to be more.

I say: Turn his head. His head in bed. You'll have no more. No more snore.

Now, there are plenty of good reasons to end a marriage, but each time I hear of another impending divorce I can't help but reevaluate my own marriage. Do I want more? Does he? And how do I know if what I have is enough?

When the van finally arrives, I realize it is not the same as the one in that first picture I saw on the Web site. This is no ordinary van for transporting the elderly. It's a 4x4 Rock Crawler version, with tinted windows, a roof rack and a camper extension that explodes out the top. Built to climb rock gorges and traverse rivers, our van also features on its front bumper a cattle-guard contraption that must have been handy when plowing through herds of wildebeests in the Serengeti but is presumably unnecessary in the suburbs.

As I circle the van, trying to hide my shock, our neighbors drive by in their Taurus. The man sticks his head out the window, pumps his fist at my husband and gives a yodeling hoot of solidarity. The woman shrugs her shoulders at me, her face scrunched up, as if she's thinking, "How will this affect our property value?"

The hulking black behemoth is so big it spills out of our driveway and into the street.

"It's more of a truck than a van," my husband concedes.

"Yes," I say. "Yes, it is."

"Just give it a chance," he says.

I feel turned inside out, but it's his insides that I'm wearing on my outsides. Every time I walk out the door, it's there: 10,000 pounds of metal, gears and after-market hydraulics, announcing to the entire neighborhood that someone in this house is having a midlife crisis.

He attempts to woo me with the van's charms—the things he thinks will appeal to me: the shower, the portable toilet, the diesel engine.

The diesel engine! Diesels can go a million miles, he claims, and in a pinch they can run on corn and potatoes. The downside to diesel is that we can barely hear one another above the roar of the engine, and communication with Ben, who seems to be about eight feet behind us in the backseat, is impossible.

So we develop a primitive sign language consisting of exaggerated gestures. Imaginary spoon to mouth: Are you hungry? Finger pointed at crotch: Need to go to the bathroom? Mother's head cupped in hands: Why didn't I look at that Web site more carefully?

My husband tries to bring me on board by asking for my input: "Let's talk about where to go on our first camping trip."

"What about Oregon?" Ben suggests.

"Baja?" says my husband.

"San Francisco?" I volunteer, which is ten miles away.

My husband orders maps from AAA. He sketches out routes. He talks weather and strategies for trading off on driving. He doesn't yet realize I have no intention of going anywhere in that thing. It smells of mold, plus my husband confesses that you have to empty the toilet by hand.

"What's the point of a Porta Potti if you have to clean it out every time you use it?" I ask, trying not to gag.

"It's for emergencies. Like if we're stuck on the highway in a blizzard."

"Why would we be stuck on the highway in a blizzard?"

"That's the whole point. That we could be stuck in a blizzard. Wouldn't that be fun? We'd be the only ones on the highway all cozy and warm."

Because everybody else, he fails to add, would have listened to the weather forecast and stayed home.

Eventually I have to tell him: "I'm not coming on the camping trip."

"You want us to go without you? Seriously?"

"Yes." What I really mean is: *No, I don't want you to go without me, but I don't want to go where you're going.*

My husband and son continue the trip discussions without me. They decide their inaugural camping trip will consist of a Saturday night in Point Reyes, about fifty miles from our house. One last invitation is extended, and I politely decline. Finally I am off the hook.

The morning of their expedition I climb into the van to load it with their requested dinner supplies: hot dogs, Gummi Worms and chocolate soy milk. Reaching into the cabinet, I discover something wedged into the very back. It's a map of the Big Sioux River in South Dakota, left behind by the young man who died.

I feel strangely dislocated as I trace the blue tributaries with my finger. I imagine him looking at the map on his final day and asking himself, *Where do I go next?* He couldn't have known that "next," for him, was not going to be a very good place. But what choice did he have? Stay home?

His zest for life (or more to the point, my lack of zest) is startling to me. Is it possible I am the one having the midlife crisis?

I used to be less afraid. In the early years of our marriage, my husband and I climbed mountains, ran Class 3 rapids in a rickety canoe and camped along the way. On rainy nights we slept in a tent, and on starry nights we slept outside. We were in our twenties; our needs were simple.

We lived dangerously, which is to say we were up for anything. We didn't think about what things cost. We thought only about the cost of not doing things. Which is exactly why—I suddenly understand—my husband has bought the van for us.

And then, just as suddenly, news of Ben's rescheduled soccer tournament ends the excursion—for the moment, at least. But there is no stopping my boys; they decide to simply camp in the driveway.

From the window, I watch them depart. Ben is beside himself with excitement, clutching his pillow, his Nintendo DS pressed to his chest like a Bible. He looks as if he is going to the moon. They wave to me as they climb aboard. Soon I hear the *whoomp-whoomp* of a bass and shrieks of laughter—they are having a dance party.

I've hardly had a night to myself since my son was born. Back in the house I pour myself a glass of wine and eat my Burmese takeout. Later, stretched out in bed, surrounded by stacks of books and magazines, I revel in my creature comforts. But as the hours pass, a vague unease settles over me, an odd kind of claustrophobia that isn't about the physical space I'm in, but the sheltered life I'm living.

Sometime after midnight, I finally push aside the covers, grab my pillow and drag myself from my warm bed. Outside, the chilly air smells of eucalyptus and toasted marshmallows. In the distance an owl hoots. I know the mattress will be stiff, the headroom cramped, and I won't sleep. But I open the van door and climb in anyway. The two people I love most in the world are out here, along with the promise of a richer, more adventurous life.

Once we leave the driveway, that is.

The misc is piling up all over again," says Ben the next morning.

He's hanging upside down like a bat from what is optimistically referred to as the van's penthouse bed.

It takes me a moment to realize he's talking about the miscellaneous folder I made for him, in which I've told him to stuff all his schoolwork that he doesn't quite know what to do with but he might need sometime in the future.

"Well, that's good," I say. "That's what the folder is for—to contain the misc so it's not floating around in your head."

"What's good about that?" says my husband.

Recently I confessed to him that I was feeling stressed and, well, a little down. He told me he wasn't surprised. I just had to get organized. All I needed was two lists: A for personal and Z for work. Then I needed to rank things according to importance. For instance, he proposed, A-1 might be having sex five times a week. A-25 might be purchasing that Mulberry bag. I told him I had a list already, thank you very much, and all I needed was a highlighter to know what task I needed to accomplish next. And it's true. I do have a list. The same list I print out every week that has had the same things highlighted for the past five years: finish household catastrophe plan (earthquake, fire, avian bird flu, mudslide), begin using meat as condiment rather than as main course, explore the possibility I may have ADD.

"Hey, Ben," my husband says, "would you like me to help you get organized? I have a system that will make you feel a lot less anxious about all that misc."

"No, thank you," says Ben.

My husband sighs. "Latte?" he says to me.

Hurrah! Our camping trip is over!

"Great idea," I say. "But let's take the Subaru to Peet's. It's so hard to find parking. You wouldn't want anybody to ding this little beauty."

"Relax. We can have a latte right here," says my husband. "If you'll just move your arm and your leg and your butt about ten inches to the left, I can make one for you."

"How about if I get out and stand in the driveway?" I say. "How would that be?"

Being with the people you love most in the world is not the same as being trapped in a van with the people you love most in the world.

I think my problem is more than just the van. I think my problem is vehicles of all kinds. I am not a person who should be allowed behind the wheel. I go a little crazy. For instance, when I am alone in the car here are some of the secret things I say:

—What the fuck, buddy?

—Could you go any slower, lady?

—Drive much, asshole?

For the record, only in the car do I call people *buddy* and *lady* and *asshole*. I think it's an East Coast thing. My friend Renee, who is from New Jersey, says *buddy* and *lady* and *asshole*, too.

"I have to pee and I'm not using the Porta Potti," I say to my husband.

"I'm peeing in the bushes," says Ben.

"Go use the bathroom and come right back out and your latte will be ready," says my husband.

His eyes are glazed, intent on the task at hand. He looks—well, he looks high. I know this look. He's in love. With his van.

When I first met my husband he drove a beat-up old Saab with the license plate KEEMO. I asked him if this was an alternate spelling for *chemo,* as he had just survived a bout with skin cancer, but he grinned and said, "Keemo-Saab-ay—get it?"

Kemo Sabe. A friend or trusted scout. How he adored that car. I should have known what was coming.

Sometimes I think my husband married the wrong woman. There are women who would love this van. Wives who would want nothing more than to hop in it with no notice and live the 4x4 lifestyle and bathe in a contraption called a sun shower every few days. Instead he has me. I know nothing about cars and the little I do know I instantly forget. Like how to open the hood. I can never find that little black lever and I'm always in a panic when I'm trying to locate it because the only time I look for it is when the car has broken down.

Now, I am not inept in all car matters. I am an excellent parallel parker. I know exactly which lines move the fastest at the tollbooths and I weave my way in and out of traffic aggressively and artfully. I am sloppy, though. I don't check the air pressure in my tires and I tend to ignore the squeals and creaks and leaks that are precursors to the engine's warning light going on, leading to the car belching steam and the AAA guy glaring at me while waiting for me to figure out how to pop the hood. He might also be giving me dirty looks because my car is a pigsty. It's one of the few places in my life where I allow myself to be a slob. About twice a year I bring it to the car wash. Yes, mine is the car that says PLEASE WASH ME! on the back window, etched in the dust by somebody's finger—a man's finger, no doubt.

My needs are simple. I just want a car that goes when I start it. Well, really what I want is a GPS. Well, *really* what I want is a woman with a kind voice who tells me when to turn left, when to turn right and who applauds me when I arrive at my final destination.

My bad car juju started with my father's brand-new 1972 Lincoln Continental. It was burgundy and had seats the color of meat. The leather was cool and smooth. It was pebbly and so much fun to lick and bite. And so I bit a chunk of leather right off my mother's headrest. That she was sitting in the seat at the time was one mistake. My other mistake was that I was far too old to be chewing on car upholstery. I can't remember my punishment, but I'm sure that it had something to do with being forced to eat a big steak, which may not sound like a punishment to you, but I assure you it was for me when I was nine.

Then right after I got my driver's permit came the episode with the Plymouth Valiant. The gas pedal got stuck. I circled the block once and my parents waved gaily at me. They waved a little less gaily the second time I came barreling around. The third time when they heard me shouting, "Help, help, I can't stop!" they looked exasperated.

"Turn the engine off!" yelled my father.

I had no idea how to do that. Was there some sort of emergency turn-the-engine-off switch?

"How?" I screamed.

My father mimed turning the key in the ignition and I followed his directions and the car sputtered to a stop.

He frequently brings up this story at Thanksgiving.

The thing about calls to adventure is you change your mind about them. At midnight they sound pretty good. At seven in the morning they are the dumbest idea you ever had. As soon as I go into the house I hate the van all over again.

And so I loiter. I brush my teeth. Throw in a load of laundry. I feel like a fugitive. At any moment I expect the front door to be kicked open and my husband to be standing there with a mug in hand. "Could you go any slower, lady?" he'll say.

The misc is piling up all over again. I need to follow my husband's advice. I just need to get organized. I'll accomplish something on my list. How about attacking that catastrophe plan? Maybe that is why I've been feeling stuck.

HOW TO KNOW IF YOUR HOUSE IS ON FIRE

1. Your husband says: I smell smoke. Do you smell smoke? I smell smoke.

2. You say: That's my new Hermès perfume. It's vetiver mixed with cigar-flavored notes of tonka bean. When it dries down it smells like Apple Jacks.

3. He sniffs your wrist and says: No, I smell smoke. I'm certain that's smoke.

4. Your son comes running into the room, tears streaming down

his face, and says: The TV blew up and is on fire. My Wii is hung. Could somebody please come reboot it before I lose my game?

WHAT TO DO WHEN YOUR HOUSE IS ON FIRE

1. Run around in circles saying: What do we do? What do we do?
2. Try to remember the lyrics to the What to Do If There's a Fire song your son learned when he was a toddler.
3. Remember only one line of one verse: Call out for help and never hide.
4. Yell: Help! Help! at the dog while jumping up and down in front of the window.

Our friend Clyde is a firefighter. Actually he's a fire captain. He says the same thing every time he comes for dinner. "Holy shit, if there's a fire in the canyon you're screwed."

Yes, we are stupid people who live at the top of a canyon. Yes, we live in the Oakland Hills, and yes, these are the same Oakland Hills that were ravaged in the Oakland Hills Firestorm of 1991 that at its peak destroyed one house every eleven seconds. But not our hill. Not our canyon. That is what I say when Mr. Fire Captain comes to dinner.

He shakes his head and says, "If there's a fire just get out."

"Out to where?" I ask.

"Just grab Ben and run down the street."

"Well, run where?"

"Away from the fucking fire," he says. "Is there something wrong with you?"

Yes, there is something wrong with me. I'm a procrastinator

when it comes to disasters. I'm of the "lightning doesn't strike twice in the same place so stand there and hope for the best" camp. I'm also of the dirty-looks-can-change-people's-behavior camp. I'm the only one in this camp at the present moment, but I'm hoping to recruit additional members.

I march out to the van with a pen and a notebook.

"You're absolutely right," I say to my husband. "I need to be more organized. You, too, buster," I say to Ben. "You know, Dad's really good at this kind of stuff. We should listen to him."

"Your latte got cold," my husband says, "so I drank it."

"We need to make a fire evacuation plan," I tell him.

"Right now?" he says.

"We need two ways out of every room."

"What about the pantry?" says Ben.

He's a sharp kid. The pantry *is* a problem. One, because he spends so much time in there staring at the shelves, wondering what to eat and wondering who's going to make it for him and then getting all depressed because his mother is incapable of whipping up a marvelous dinner out of tomato paste, canned pineapple and bread crumbs, and two, because it's basically a closet and there are no windows, no other way to get out except for the door, which could very well be ablaze because his mother forgot to turn the burner off and melted the Teflon nonstick coating off the frying pan once again.

"From now on, limit your time in the pantry," I say. "No more than two minutes."

"Smoke alarms?" says my husband.

"We've got 'em!" I say.

"Yes, I know we have them, but when's the last time you checked the batteries?"

"There are no batteries. Remember, we took them out because the alarms kept going off every time somebody took a shower?"

Ben begins to sing. "I have a song to share with you. I have a song to share with you. If you should ever see a fire. Here are some things that you should do."

"Good boy!" I cry. It's that safety song he learned as a toddler. I hadn't remembered it being such a catchy little ditty.

He continues. "And if your clothes should catch on fire. And if your clothes should catch on fire. You must stay calm and don't start running. You need to stop and drop and roll. Yes, if your clothes should catch on fire. You need to stop and drop and roll."

We all look at each other silently, imagining the youngest member of our family combusting. Ben climbs into my lap. My husband fiddles around with the stereo dial.

"This," I say, "is exactly why this has been on my to-do list for five years."

"I know it's hard, but we have to think about these things. We need an escape plan," says my husband.

"Okay. Let's escape, then," I say.

"Finally," he says.

He starts the van and we pull out of the driveway.

It's Sunday morning and the village is crowded. My husband has to drive around three times before he finds a parking space big enough to fit the van in. I tilt my captain's seat way back so nobody can see me as he expertly reverses and forwards his way into the tight space. I shut my eyes.

"Wake me when you've parked," I say.

Once we're situated my husband pops the van's penthouse top and sets up a game of Boggle.

"We're camping in the village!" says Ben.

"And we didn't even have to get a permit," says my husband. "See—this baby is already paying for itself."

Every few minutes a man raps on the window and says, "What the hell is this thing?"

Then my husband patiently explains about the Quigley suspension, how it can drive over boulders and could most certainly drive through a firestorm. Ben feels better and better. I feel better and better. I can go home and cross "Fire" off the catastrophe-planning section of my to-do list. The van is our catastrophe plan. We stay there for so long, holding court, that we get hungry and I have to leave again for more provisions.

As soon as I get out a woman accosts me.

"Shame on you, lady," she says, glaring at the van taking up two parking spaces. "How can you drive that thing? People are dying for oil."

"Yes, well," I tell her. "It runs on French fries."

"It runs on the oil they fry the French fries in," shouts my husband from inside the van.

The woman gives me a dirty look. I shrug my shoulders. And just like that my bad car juju is over.

October

THE NIGHT BEFORE HALLOWEEN BEN TELLS ME HE IS TOO OLD TO BE A NINJA. Unfortunately for him I am too old to be running out to Target on a Tuesday night to get him a new costume. But I see his point. I saw it a month ago when he first modeled the costume for me. The sight of his nine-year-old, nearly five-foot-tall body swaddled in royal blue polyester and wreathed in swords was heartbreaking. I didn't know whether to laugh or weep. I did neither, of course. I tried to keep an encouraging look on my face because I knew in his soul he *was* a ninja: pure, with an incorruptible code of honor.

"Darn," I say, looking at my watch. "It's seven. Target's closed."

"That's okay," he says. "You can make me a costume. I'd like to be an iPod. We just need some cardboard."

"Cardboard?" I say, trying to imagine it.

"And some Super Glue," he adds, parsing the is-this-kid-serious look on my face, watching his dream slip away.

"Wait—I know!" I say. "I've got another costume."

"You do?" Perhaps I'm not some lazy, lying, un-crafty mother.

"Yes, it's in my bedroom. Let me go get it."

"Wait. Is it in a bag?" he asks.

"What do you mean, is it in a bag?"

"Is it still in the plastic?" he asks.

Oh. He wants to know if it's new. "It's been airing out," I tell him.

"For how long?"

"Well, for a while," I confess.

"You were saving it for me?"

"Kind of," I say.

"Since when?"

"Since—college?"

He slumps as if I have just beaten him across the shoulders with a cane. "You want me to wear your costume from college?"

"Just try it," I say. "If you don't like it we'll go to Target."

"You said Target's closed."

"Well, usually it's closed by now," I say. "But they probably have special Halloween hours. I just remembered that."

He looks at me with enlightened ninja eyes and shakes his head.

I do not understand all this Halloween hoopla. Every year it gets worse. The celebrations begin weeks before the actual day. We have already been to three parties and a trick-or-treat dress rehearsal in the cul-de-sac up the street (just in case the children have forgotten how to stick out their greedy little paws), and now tomorrow is the all-school Halloween parade, and then at dusk the real madness begins.

I call my twin sister, Dawn. She is my Oracle. I always call her when I need advice on anything kid-related. She has been through it all and she's not one of those rigid mothers. For instance, when her twin boys were toddlers they were strict vegetarians. She would feed them perfect little squares of tofu and cherry tomatoes and, for snacks, almonds and olives. Then a few years passed and she had a third boy and now their cupboards and freezer are stuffed with every junk food product imaginable: Toaster Strudels, Cap'n Crunch, Hot Pockets. I love her for this. Truly I do. Every time she opens the cupboards she gives a little groan. Being twins, we have a special kind of bond. Not telepathy, but close—an entire secret vocabulary of sighs. This particular back-of-the-throat twittering means *If you had three boys you'd buy this crap, too, Melanie, so shut the hell up.* Then she grabs some Chips Ahoy!

Every once in a while I can't resist saying to her, "Remember when the boys were vegetarians?" She says, "Remember when you tried out for cheerleading in those sweatpants and your spare tampon projectiled out of your knee sock when you did a split eagle?"

When will they be too old for Halloween?" I ask the Oracle.

"Don't hold your breath," says Dawn. "I heard about this kid in eighth grade who's going as one of those new lightbulbs. You know, the kind that go for eight thousand hours and cost twenty bucks? And he actually lights up. There's a little cord on his arm that you pull. I just hope he doesn't get electrocuted," she says in a tone that tells me she very much hopes he gets electrocuted.

"What is that mother thinking?" I say, envisioning the candy.

At least there's that. At least there'll be Almond Joys at the end of it all.

Ben does not want to be a jailbird.

"What kind of a kid dresses as a prisoner for Halloween?" he says when he sees the black-and-white-striped bottoms, top and beanie, which looked so cute and sexy on my twenty-year-old self. (It was 1983. I think I may have also worn pink leg warmers and pumps in addition to the jailbird costume. In my defense *Flashdance* had just come out. It was a good year—everywhere I went people told me I looked like Jennifer Beals.)

"Cool kids," I tell him. "*Tough* kids."

He tries it on.

"You look fabulous," I say.

"No—I don't," he says, throwing the beanie at me.

"I have another idea," I say.

A long, long time ago we had a New Year's Eve party. This was back in the days when we were capable of staying up until midnight. Now that we live in California we celebrate what we call an East Coast New Year's. Which means we go to bed at nine and call it good. Anyway, one of the many wonderful qualities my husband has (and I seem to lack) is what you might call joie de vivre—and for this New Year's Eve party he bought twelve amazing hats (over $400 worth!) for our guests to wear. They were Dr. Seussian affairs: whimsical with dangly, curlicue things and all of them nearly a foot high. There was a Christmas tree. A basket of fruit. One of those hats is just what this costume needs.

"Where's the angel hat?" I ask Ben.

Panic darkens his face.

"I'm serious. Go find it. You're going to be a fallen angel," I say.

"No," he says.

"Yes," I say. "A fallen angel. An angel who's been booted out of heaven and is now in jail. I guarantee you nobody else will have the same costume."

"When's Dad coming home?" asks Ben.

I find the hat. It's white and fluffy with gold wings. I position it on his head so it dips over one eye, like a fedora. Now he looks like a gangster fallen angel.

"I can't see," he tells me.

"It's literary," I say. "It's ironic."

Honestly, he looks a little like Truman Capote, but I don't tell him that.

"Nobody will get it," he says.

I sigh. "We'll make a sign."

I am a crafty and industrious mother, after all. I get a piece of cardboard. I stab a hole in it with a kitchen knife. I lace through some twine and in big block letters I write FALLEN ANGEL on the cardboard. I then place this sign around my son's neck. He races to go look at himself in the mirror.

"Really?" he says.

I can see the idea slowly growing on him.

"Really," I say. "Trust me. It's perfect."

And it is perfect until ten that night when I'm lying in bed and it occurs to me that having a FALLEN ANGEL in the school's Halloween parade might offend a few people—a few people of the Christian persuasion.

I call my friend Robin. What you need to know about Robin is that she's Jewish. And a cabaret singer. And a therapist for children. Recently she conducted a Life Skills workshop at my son's school. Because she is my friend I admitted to her that I, too, was in need of some Life Skills. So she shared this relaxation exercise with me.

THE BIRTHDAY CANDLE BREATHING ROUTINE

- Breathe in through your nose to the count of 2.
- Hold your breath for the same count of 2.
- Release your breath through your nose and your mouth, to the count of 4. Pretend you are slowly blowing out your birthday candles! As you are blowing, think a positive thought. Example: "I am okay," or "This isn't so bad," or "He/she is mad at me, but that doesn't mean EVERYONE is."

I've found doing this routine while sitting in the car pool line at school to be very effective.

"So will the Gentiles be mad if Ben is a Fallen Angel for Halloween?" I ask Robin.

"You're a Gentile," she reminds me.

"Yes, but the last time we were in church was when Ben was baptized."

"Hmm," she says. "Why do you think it would piss them off?"

"Because they don't like their angels to fall? Because he'll also be dressed like the Birdman of Alcatraz?"

"You didn't say that. So your son's going to be an incarcerated angel?"

"He's wrongly imprisoned, of course," I offer. "Wrongly tossed out. Of, you know—*heaven.*"

There's that word again. It's hard for me to say "heaven." Yes, I am a Gentile. Yes, I spent four years as a counselor at the Episcopal Conference Center in Rhode Island where we went to church twice a day, but I'm not sure I believe in heaven. I want to, though. I really want to. Especially now that I have a child. Maybe forcing my son to be a Fallen Angel for Halloween is a step toward that. I sniffle.

"Are you *crying?*" asks my husband, who's lying beside me in bed.

"Target's still open," says Robin and hangs up.

There's this strange phenomenon. An hour after you've put your children to sleep, the ways in which you have wronged them sprawl out on your chest, all two hundred and fifty pounds of them, and suck the breath right out of you. It works the same way with gratitude. An hour after your family has left the house, you love them with a piercing intensity that was nowhere to be found when you were scraping egg yolk off their breakfast dishes. Your hope is to one day feel this way about them when they're in the room. This is a pretty lofty goal.

"I'm not crying," I say.

"Oh—okay," says my husband, handing me a tissue.

"We are horrible parents," I say. "Why don't we take Ben to church?"

"We did. But he cried the whole time, so we left," says my husband.

"That was nine years ago. He was an infant. They were flicking water at him."

"The priest didn't flick, he dribbled, and it was holy water."

My husband knows better than to have a conversation like this at ten at night. He rolls over.

I poke him in the middle of the back. "I have to lose some weight. We have to go on a diet tomorrow."

"Fine," he mutters.

"I'm serious."

"Okay."

I begin sniffling again. "Don't you want to know why?"

My husband groans. "Why?" he asks.

"Ben told me there was no way God could carry me up to heaven. I'm too fat."

It dawns on me the next day, as I'm sitting in the bleachers in the gymnasium at my son's school, that I've lost my edge. I'm watching the lower school parade by in their costumes, and I have no idea what these kids are supposed to be.

Oh, she's a roll of toilet paper. No, she's a marshmallow.

Oh, he's an ice cube. No, he's global warming.

Ooo-la-la, she's a French maid. No, she's Alice in Wonderland.

If only their mothers had made them signs to wear around their necks. If only all of us wore signs around our necks that announced to everybody who we were. Wouldn't we be a lot less confused?

Ben is wearing the prison costume. I've made him another sign. This one says DEPARTMENT OF CORRECTIONS PRISONER #328459. I'm so proud of him. I think his costume is just right given his age. It doesn't look like he worked too hard on it (a plus in my book), and he looks cool.

When I was a kid I was a clown for Halloween. What I mean is that I was a clown *every year* for Halloween. It was the only option available to me, as Dawn was always a cowgirl and Rebecca, my older sister, was always a witch. At least this is how I remember it. Sara, my youngest sister, was not born yet so she was not a part of this triumvirate. That there was something else to be besides clown, cowgirl and witch never occurred to me.

I was not a person who took risks. I'd start thinking about my costume in the summer. Wonder what I'll be this year? How about a clown? Maybe a clown? Think I'll be a clown. Truthfully, all the other costumes scared me. When I was nine I believed that the costume you wore sank into you. This was serious stuff. You were choosing who you were going to be. Your costume was your destiny. I watch my son race around the gym, and I see his destiny: his ninja heart, which is no longer safe to show the world; his iPod bones, which he's chosen for aesthetics and entertainment purposes and which I've rejected; and his jailbird skin, which I'm in the process of tattooing permanently onto his body.

I wish I could tell you that when we leave school we drive straight to Target and I buy my son the perfect costume, but this is not a fairy tale. Instead, I go home and climb into bed. I feel like a bride on the morning of her wedding day: pumped full of adrenaline yet fatigued to the point of exhaustion, and the big moment, the big I DO, is yet to come.

A few minutes later Ben climbs into bed with me. I know one day he will be too old to snuggle, but thank God that day hasn't arrived yet. He doesn't let me touch him in public anymore, but here in the bowels of our house, in the sanctuary of our bed, it's safe to throw his legs over mine and let me stroke the hair back from his temple. This is what I'm best at—being his safe place.

Lying in bed, my limbs entangled with his, his feet nearly as big as mine on the eve of what will certainly be the last Halloween I will have any say over what he wants to be, I am light-headed. The day feels stuffed with too many molecules—it's as if summer, spring, winter and fall have been crammed into one afternoon. I nuzzle Ben's head.

"Stop smelling me," he says.

Usually this kind of smelling leads to me telling him to take a shower, which is a very bad outcome for a kid.

"It's Halloween," he reminds me. "Are you going to make me take a shower?"

"No, not today," I say.

"Tomorrow?"

"Not tomorrow either."

"When?"

"How about the day after that?"

Ben presses his hand against mine, measuring our fingers. He's always calculating, waiting for the day when he will be bigger than me. I am waiting for the day when he takes a shower without my prompting him to. I'll be waiting a lot longer than he will.

"You're a good woman," he says.

It sounds like something he's lifted from *The Waltons,* a show he watches from time to time. Imagine living on your own mountain, having a passel of brothers and sisters who wish you no harm, walking down a lovely dirt road to school, your books tied together in a neat little bundle with a shoelace. *You're a good woman, Livie,* Pa Walton would say to Ma Walton when she made a pound of beef feed twelve people. This is Ben's way of saying it's okay I didn't make him into an iPod because I have other qualities, like letting him go three days without bathing.

Here's how Halloween works in Northern California. One enthusiastic mother agrees to host. The other mothers bring the kids over at 5:00 p.m. and by 5:05 the drinking is well under way.

The spouses arrive around six and soon after take the kids out for trick-or-treating, Dixie cups of scotch sloshing around in their hands. The mothers eat cookies shaped like witches' fingers and say things like: *Jesus, I've already gained ten pounds, and once I found out I had elevated blood sugar levels everything made sense: my constantly being angry, my backing the Volvo into that stone wall, the endless thirst!*

Halloween's almost over, is what I'm thinking, while watching the clock. Soon I can go back to a normal life.

When the kids return they race upstairs to examine their loot. We continue to pound down the Sauvignon Blanc, but after about half an hour it occurs to me that they're oddly quiet. A few minutes later Ben comes downstairs and sits next to me on the couch.

"I'm ready to go home," he says.

He isn't dressed like a prisoner anymore. He's stripped down to his jeans and T-shirt. In a fit of creativity, before we left the house I gave him a black eye with some face paint. Prisoners are always getting in fights, aren't they? The entire left side of his face is now the color of a prune.

"Me, too," I say to him. "Get your candy and let's go."

"I don't have any candy," he says.

"What do you mean you don't have any candy?"

"I gave it away."

"Why would you give your candy away?"

"Because I didn't want it," he says softly.

"We'll see about that," I say, grabbing him by the hand and marching him upstairs.

He's been swindled out of his candy! This is exactly why I

insisted he be a criminal for Halloween. So he could stand up to bullies!

"Please, don't," he says.

"No way, buster," I say. "This is unacceptable."

Up in the bedroom I find what I think is a pirate, a ghost, P. Diddy and what I can only surmise is Alan Greenspan (but don't quote me on that) sitting in front of four heaping piles of candy. Looking at that candy I am furious.

"What's happened here?" I demand of the boys. "Where is Ben's candy?"

"He gave it to us," says the pirate, shrugging.

"Now why would he do that?" I say.

A mother steps forward. "It's true," she says. "I saw him. He gave it away."

A father says, "This is great! Aren't you happy about this? Why, it's every parent's dream. I wish my kid would give away all his candy. Besides, it's better for you. Less temptation. Tomorrow, I mean. We all know who ends up eating the candy."

"You don't understand," I say. "I'm afraid he'll regret this."

Ben looks up at me with his big green eyes pleading silently for me to let it go. But I can't. Something is horribly, horribly wrong.

"Sweetheart," I say, "how are you going to feel in the morning when you have no candy? Do you understand what's happening here? You're going to wake up in the morning and have NO CANDY."

"Well," he says, "I do like Almond Joys."

The pirate, the ghost, P. Diddy and Alan Greenspan hurl their Almond Joys gleefully at us. What the hell kind of kid likes

Almond Joys? Well, a kid with a mother on the warpath who likes Almond Joys.

"There—all settled," says P. Diddy's mother.

We go downstairs and say our good-byes and I feel shaky, as if we have just narrowly escaped being in a car accident.

"Don't be mad at me," says Ben.

"I'm not mad," I say. "I just don't understand."

But I am mad. I'm disappointed. Why doesn't Ben stick up for himself? How is he going to make it in the world?

"You don't know what it was like," he says. "Ask Dad."

"Dad's already gone home."

"Well, he saw it," says Ben.

"Saw what?"

"They had no Halloween spirit!" Ben cries. "They just raced from house to house getting candy. They didn't even say thank you. They didn't even stop to look at the decorations. I couldn't keep the candy. It just felt bad. Bad, bad, bad!" he says.

There comes a time in every mother's life when it becomes very clear that your child is a much better person than you are, but you're not allowed to say this because then where would you go from there—admitting such a thing to a nine-year-old?

ACTIVITY: ROLE PLAYING

DIRECTIONS: Two people play at a time. The two actors decide on a real-life drama that includes two characters and a situation. For example:

• Two people on vacation when their car runs out of gas.
• A door-to-door salesperson trying to sell you a kangaroo.

• Two people who haven't seen each other in a long time walk up and greet one another.

Do you know sometimes when you look at your kid and it's like his face has run away? Suddenly he no longer belongs to you? And for a moment you can imagine him free in the world, living, loving and dying without you ever knowing him? Without you ever having spoken one true thing to him?

"Your goodness dazzles me," I tell him.

The roads are dark. The air smells of jasmine and moon. Parents become children and children become parents. The membrane between life and death stretches thinner every day, but still we are rich. We have eight Almond Joys. We tear them open and gobble them down.

November

FORTY-FOUR. WHAT KIND OF NOTHING AGE IS FORTY-FOUR? I CALL DAWN TO commiserate.

"How did this happen?" I say when she picks up the phone.

"Hmm," she says, which is twin-speak for what kind of nothing age is forty-four?

"It adds up to eight," I say. "That's got to be a good thing. Isn't eight some kind of important number?"

"Oh, sure," she says. "It's one year past the seven-year itch."

"Speaking of sevens, it's seventy degrees here," I tell her.

It's impossible to be a New Englander and live in California and not feel smug during the winter months.

"Is it cold there in Cohasset? It must be really cold," I say.

I hear her breathing.

"Dawn?"

"What?"

"I miss the cold."

"Screw you," she says. "We're doing Chinese food and a movie."

That's what I usually want for my birthday. At least that's what I say I want. Of course, that's code for I want so much more but I'm not going to tell you what I want because you should just *know* and if you don't get it for me I'll be really mad.

"You're the only one who called on my birthday," Dawn says.

"You, too!" I cry.

We have the same conversation every year—the poor-forgotten-overlooked-twins conversation. It's our mythology and we cling to it like a blankie. Here's how it works: in our family of four girls, the oldest and the youngest are not only the most beloved but also the smartest, the most popular and the ones with the best hair. Those unlucky enough to have been born in the middle—just two minutes apart—have only each other.

Take for instance when we were ten. Dawn had a cold, so my mother kept her home from school. I missed her so much I told my friends she had fallen off an eight-foot-high stone wall and broken her leg and now she was in the hospital.

I may have elaborated further. She was lying on the ground groaning in pain for hours, clutching her leg, the bone sticking straight out of her calf before I found her—my unfortunate, left-for-dead twin sister. When the teacher got wind of this she stopped our math lesson and had everybody spend the rest of the period making cards for Dawn. I made one for her, too, with an illustration of her falling off the wall and a little speech bubble that said, "Help, Melanie, help!"

When I got home from school Dawn was eating a 3 Musketeers Bar and watching *The Love Boat* in the living room. My parents were very strict. We were only allowed candy on Sundays. Sundays were candy day, not Tuesdays. I took the cards out of my knapsack and threw them at her.

"Here," I said.

"What's this?" asked my mother.

"The kids made Dawn cards."

"Why?" said my mother.

"Because she's sick."

"With the sniffles?"

"Well—yes," I said. "They were worried."

My mother rifled through the cards, a look of growing horror on her face.

—I hope you get out of the hospital real soon.

—One day you'll walk again!!!

—Good thing Melody found you.

"Help, Dawn, help!" I shouted as my mother grabbed me by the elbow and hustled me from the room to begin a six-month sentence of punishments.

"Happy Birthday to us," I sing to Dawn.

I can hear her boys screaming in the background. She sighs and then the phone goes dead.

My husband, a surfer, is in the garage soaking his wet suits in a pail.

"I changed my mind. I don't want to go out for Chinese food."

"Okay," he says. "What do you want?"

"I want something good. Something homemade. Something that you would eat on a cold November day."

"Like scalloped potatoes?" asks my husband.

"Yes, but with cheese."

"Au gratin potatoes?"

I nod.

"What else?"

"Lamb. Leg of lamb," I say.

"And éclairs from La Farine," he finishes.

"That would be nice, but I don't need éclairs *and* a cake," I say.

He swishes the wet suits around with a pole. He swishes the wet suits around with a pole some more.

"You didn't get me a cake?" I say.

"You said you didn't want a cake."

"And you believed me?"

"Let's go shopping," he says cheerily.

"You go shopping," I say. "I'll stay home."

I have an aversion to grocery stores. I hate them. Just pulling into the parking lot causes my blood pressure to spike.

"No, you're coming with us," he says. "It's your birthday and you just talked to your sister and you're homesick and you're not staying here alone."

"Fine. As long as we don't have to take the van."

The only thing worse than going to the grocery store is going to the grocery store in the van.

Because I need to replenish my almond supply I suggest we go to Trader Joe's.

Almonds are the thing I eat when what I really want to eat is Kozy Shack rice pudding. I keep bags of almonds everywhere: in my car, in my purse and in various locations in the house. They are a very effective appetite suppressant. The key, I've found, is to eat enough of them. A handful is not enough. One cup will not only take the edge off but will make you feel just the teensiest bit sick, so the thought of scarfing down a quart-size container of rice pudding is no longer desirable.

In addition to the almonds we get our leg of lamb and some nice Yukon Gold potatoes and a bottle of birthday wine. My husband was right. I needed to get out of the house. It's so festive in the store. The aisles are sun-splashed and the staff gives away free samples of oatmeal raisin cookies and pomegranate lemonade.

"Not everybody has Trader Joe's," I say to my husband.

For instance, there is no Trader Joe's in Cohasset.

"It's your birthday," he whispers in my ear. "And I'm going to make you a nice birthday dinner."

We have been traveling down the aisles with a woman and her two young children. This woman has long, gray, ponytailed hair and has a kind of a hippie cool-Berkeley-mom vibe going (she's wearing a sleeveless tunic over jeans), and she smiles at me the kind of smile that says *Aren't we lucky we live in this great part of the country where it's seventy degrees at the end of November and look at my vibrant, unscheduled, wildly creative Waldorf children who have never watched TV, never picked up a Nintendo DS, and look at your boy (what amazing green eyes—he looks nothing like you) and look at all of us with our bags of pumpkin seeds and legs of lambs and gingersnap cookies.*

I am a sucker for smiles like this, and so, besotted, I follow this woman straight into the checkout line. This, of course, is a big mistake. Because it turns out she is not just grocery-shopping, she is having a lifestyle experience. Here's what a lifestyle experience at Trader Joe's looks like:

1. You move very, very slowly.
2. You discuss your food choices and your children's allergies at length with the cashier.
3. You open a tin of chocolate-covered Altoids and distribute them to everybody in your line and the line next to yours.
4. You insist on helping the bagger, and then you bag very, very slowly.
5. When you are carded (they card EVERYBODY at Trader Joe's), you say, "You're kidding, right?" but what you mean is "You're not the only one who thinks I look twenty-two when really I'm thirty-five," and then you tell the cashier the story of how you went prematurely gray when you were twenty-two.
6. When the cashier rings you up and chirps good-bye, you look under your cart and see that you've forgotten to pay for your laundry detergent and toilet paper. "Oh, no," you cry. "Just take it," says the weary cashier.

I am also having a lifestyle experience. Here's what my lifestyle experience at Trader Joe's on my forty-fourth birthday looks like.

1. I huff loudly.
2. I huff even more loudly.
3. I look at the person behind me in line and roll my eyes.
4. The person behind me looks the other way because he's having a lifestyle experience similar to the gray-haired ponytail woman and he's not going to let some bitter woman who would be better off shopping at Lucky's pull him down.
5. My husband suggests I *breathe*. He tries to distract me by asking me how is it possible that I forgot Julia Child came to our house for dinner.

6. I tell him I'm sure it has something to do with the fact that he
has just been lecturing me on the proper way to prepare a leg of
lamb: cut slits in the meat and insert cloves of garlic; swat with
branches of fresh rosemary and thyme; brush with olive oil and
marinate in a nice Bordeaux.

"We have to stop at Lucky's," I say once we get in the car.

"But we just went to Trader Joe's."

"Yes, but I need rice pudding now," I say. "To recover. From
going to Trader Joe's."

"Have some almonds," says Ben from the backseat.

"No, I need rice pudding."

"What about the éclairs?" says my husband.

"You can stick a candle in rice pudding," I tell him.

"But Mom, you need forty-four candles," says Ben. "There's no
way you can fit forty-four candles in a container of rice pudding."

"Doesn't that place drive you crazy?" I say. "Does it drive anybody else crazy but me?"

Ben shrugs.

My husband says, "You were mad when she came."

"Well, could that lady have taken any longer? Did she have to
tell us about her son's shellfish allergy?"

"I was talking about Julia," says my husband.

I hate going to the grocery store because I am not a cook. Most
evenings in my house we scrounge and eat standing up around the
island. I am embarrassed about this fact, but I can't seem to do
anything about it. When dinnertime rolls around I am uninter-
ested, uninspired and usually a little bit mad.

"You were mad when she came," my husband recalls, as we pull out of the Trader Joe's parking lot. "You seemed really irritated."

"Why would I be irritated that Julia came to our house for dinner? People would die to have Julia Child come to their home. They would pay a lot of money for that," I say. "Like if they won dinner with her. In an auction," I clarify.

He frowns. "I don't know, but you were," he says.

A few minutes later I ask him what I served. If Julia Child came to your house for dinner you really should know what you served.

Some people can recall in detail the wild nettle frittata they ate for dinner one Indian summer night in 1972. I don't understand these people. It's not that I wouldn't like to be one of them, but I just don't see it happening this late in my life. Food is just not that important to me.

"I made homemade fettuccine with lobster and scallops," he says proudly. "And fresh asparagus. With a little lemon. Clarified butter."

"Hmm," I say.

"She loved it," he says.

The evening Julia came for dinner slowly returns to me, but certain things are fuzzy. Did I voluntarily cede the kitchen over to my husband? Or was I pushed out? And, really, does it matter? What *would* I have made if dinner had been left to me? This was 1995. What were my specialties back then? Well, most likely the same as my specialties now. Lasagna. Egg noodles with butter and Parmesan. Turkey burgers and corn on the cob.

"Did you forget that she came to our engagement dinner, too?" he asks.

"Of course not," I say, but I had forgotten that as well.

Something is wrong here. I seem to have some sort of food-related amnesia. And the problem is I am hungry. My family is hungry.

We didn't win a dinner with Julia Child at an auction. The reason she came to our house was because she had known my husband since he was a boy: my husband's grandmother was one of Julia's good friends. When my husband was fifteen he lived on and off at her home in Cambridge. The very house where she filmed her TV show. Once he made fish tacos with her in Santa Barbara and afterward they did tai chi on the beach. And yes, she came to our engagement party, although I have little recollection of that.

When we get home I throw the bags of almonds into a drawer and plop down on the couch with my tub of rice pudding and a spoon.

My husband listens to voice mail. "Your sisters and your mother called to wish you Happy Birthday," he says. "Also Robin. She said put the rice pudding down now."

"She did not say that," I say.

He hands me the phone. I listen to the messages and weep. I forget every year that my mother and sisters call.

I call Robin back.

"How's the birthday girl?"

"I think I have a grocery store phobia," I tell her. "You know, the way some people can't drive over bridges or highways?"

"So order online. Have your food delivered."

"No, you don't understand. I don't cook for my family. We just stand around the island and eat."

Robin sighs. "It's tough living in Aliceland," she says.

She's talking about Alice Waters. The Bay Area is home to Alice Waters's legendary restaurant, Chez Panisse. You can't go anywhere in this town and not hear talk of her, the high priestess of organically grown and simply prepared food. I chaperoned Ben on a field trip to the UC Botanical Gardens the other week and there was a whole garden dedicated to Alice.

"Nasturtiums!" announced the docent (Alice uses them in her salad!).

"Squash blossoms!" (Alice fries them up in a little salt and organic butter!)

"Tomatillos! (Alice dices them up and sautés them with caramelized onions!)

In Aliceland, the children eat organic Ho Hos (if they must eat them at all, and Alice would rather they wouldn't) and their parents shop at farmers' markets every day like the French people do.

Most nights my husband calls around five and gently says, "Have you thought about dinner?"

This is not a sexist question, nor is it a mean one. He's simply trying to gather information. Now, there is a big difference between *What's for dinner* and *Have you thought about dinner* and that difference is pressure. My husband always leaves me an escape hatch.

"No, I haven't thought about it," I'll sigh. "I wish I had, but I haven't."

"That's all right," he says. "We'll scrounge."

And because he is a man who once did White Crane Spreads Its Wings on the beach with Julia Child, he has a certain confidence in the kitchen (which, yes, occasionally edges over into smugness, but really, can you blame him?) and he gamely comes home and scrounges for us all. His idea of scrounge is baby greens hand-tossed with an olive oil, garlic and shallot vinaigrette and a perfectly cooked eight-minute egg topped with shavings of Asiago.

He is happy to do this, but I want something different for us. I know what a pleasure it is to come home to a house redolent with the smell of dinner cooking. I also know that the heady scent of a roasting chicken is about so much more than a roasting chicken.

"I want to start bringing something besides salad for our potlucks," I tell Robin.

"You bring other things," says Robin. "Remember, you made buttercup squash soup?"

"I made buttercup squash soup?"

Besides not remembering that Julia came to our house for a meal, or my buttercup squash soup phase, I've forgotten scads of other things. Things one should remember, like how to do long division, the names of my friends' dogs, and the characters in books I've just read. Also I can't remember what I say or to whom I say it.

"We have ants," I say at breakfast. "We have ants," I say at lunch. "We have ants," I say again at dinner.

My long-term memory is even worse. I seem to have forgotten all the firsts. Who was the first boy to tell me he loved me? What did I wear on my first date with my husband? What was my son's first word?

Here are some observations I've culled about forgetting and remembering: I tend to forget in threes; I forget anything good that has ever happened to me almost immediately after it happens; I have no problem recalling every grudge, every slight and every rejection that has to do with being forgotten, overlooked or left for dead. This may be why there is no room in my brain to remember anything good.

I planned on sharing my observations with my internist when it was time for my annual physical, during the part where she asks me if I have any concerns and usually I say, no, nothing, I'm feeling great, except for this lump on the inside of my elbow, I'm sure it's nothing but maybe you should take a look—but I chickened out. I was afraid she'd suggest I had early-onset Alzheimer's or that I was a woman with too much time on her hands.

I planned on sharing my observations with my gynecologist, as the symptoms seemed more hormone-related, but I chickened out with her, too. I was afraid she'd suggest I was in early menopause or make me start keeping a gratitude journal.

I planned on taking my observations to my therapist, but I no longer have a therapist and I can barely remember what I talked about for the three years I was talking about it.

Luckily there are documents. Archives in the form of file drawers stuffed full of expired warranties, deeds, letters, certificates, invoices, and old paycheck stubs. These are always handy for a little trip down memory lane. By reading them I can put together a snapshot of my life.

Certificate of Birth: April 30, 1998, 7:09 p.m. Baby boy, Benjamin. 8 lbs., 9 oz. 21 inches long.

Purchased: November 28, 1998. One light box. $355. Warning: For Seasonal Affective Disorder Only. Do not use for more than two hours a day or mania may occur.

Purchased: February 12, 1999. One baby swing. $259. Warning: Do not swing baby for more than fifteen minutes at a time.

Purchased: March 9, 1999. One light box. $355. Warning: For

Seasonal Affective Disorder Only. Do not use for more than two hours a day or mania may occur.

Returned: One Light Box. To Whom It May Concern: Remembered I already bought a light box. Sent back March 20, 1999. Awaiting refund.

Returned: April 12, 1999. One baby swing. To Whom It May Concern: Enclosed please find the baby swing I purchased February 12, 1999. The quality of your baby swing is very poor. I've only had it for a few months and it broke. Please send a refund to this address.

Dear Melanie Gideon: May 13, 1999. We are sorry to tell you we will not be issuing you a refund as the baby swing clearly broke due to overuse. Enclosed please find a coupon for $10 off your next purchase. P.S. Hope your kid doesn't have permanent brain damage. (No, they didn't say that, but I can read between the lines.)

I forgot Julia Child came to my house for dinner," I confess to Robin.

Robin gasps. "Jesus, what did you serve her?"

"What did we make Julia?" I shout at my husband, who's mincing garlic.

"Pasta with shrimp and lobster," shouts my husband. "I already told you that."

"Pasta with shrimp and lobster," I say.

"Fra Diablo," says Robin, sighing. "Perfect."

She's a cook. She's probably right at this moment whipping up a nice duck confit. When she has people over for dinner she starts preparing days in advance. She goes to four or five different shops: one for cheese, one for wine, one for meat and one for produce. I cannot think of a worse torture. Searching for parking four times, having to choose between this kind of Brie and that kind of Brie (having missed the memo that the new Brie is something called La Tur).

"I don't understand why I can't remember," I say to Robin. "The meal is a complete blank."

"Probably because the food wasn't what mattered to you, so it didn't stick," says Robin.

"But shouldn't I remember *something*?"

"You will," she says.

A week later I get a card in the mail from my mother—a belated birthday present. It's a gift certificate for Chez Panisse. It's a beautiful hand-letter-pressed card with an illustration of cabbage—no, collard greens—no, romaine lettuce. Just the sight of it makes me anxious, as if I have to live up to something. I immediately hide it. It's another call to adventure, but I've come to realize a call to adventure really means a call to feel really bad about yourself and all your shortcomings.

My husband finds the gift certificate.

"Chez Panisse! Wow! Let's go tonight," he says.

"It's Saturday. You can't just walk into Chez Panisse," I say. "See, it says for information and reservations call this number. It takes months to get in."

"Okay. Let's call and make a reservation for a month from now."

"Yes, let's!" I say, thinking he'll get a reservation for next summer.

He gets off the phone and grins at me. "Get your purse. We're going to Chez Panisse."

"Now?"

"Yes, now. Can you believe it? They had a cancellation."

"Yes, I can believe it—it's four forty-five in the afternoon."

"We'll drive slow," he says. "It'll be five by the time we get there."

I've found that most menus contain secret messages if you are in need of a secret message, and Chez Panisse's menu does not disappoint: **fall** vegetable salad **and** green beans, arti**choke**s and chervil steamed Atlantic cod with wild mushrooms spit-roasted **laughing stock** farm pork loin with chestnuts, celery root pu**ree** and mus**tard** greens meyer lemon meringue tartlet.

> Fall and choke
> Laughingstock
> Retard

Translation: We're on to you, you non-recycler, you buyer of Chilean grapes. You don't belong here; you'll fall off your chair and choke on a fish bone and you'll be the laughingstock of the restaurant and you may as well leave now, retard.

Now, that's not a nice way to begin a meal, and it only gets worse—at Chez Panisse I can't taste a damn thing. I sample from everybody's plate, but to my unsophisticated palate, simple and unadulterated and fresh translates into dull. There is a little dab of something green atop my cod that is the highlight of my meal. Of course, I don't say this because my son and my husband are groaning with pleasure.

It seems I forgot how to taste. How did this happen? *When* did this happen? I wasn't always this way. I remember when I was eight, eating strawberries right off the vine. It was August and so hot the berries were practically baked, and when I popped them in my mouth they bloomed, spreading across my tongue like petals.

I go back to the menu again, trying to cipher out another message: fall **vegetable** salad and green **beans**, **arti**chokes and **cher**vil **steamed** Atlantic cod with wild mushrooms **spit**-roasted laughing stock farm pork loin with chestnuts, celery **root** puree and mustard **greens** meyer lemon meringue tartlet.

> Vegetable be art
> Cher steamed
> Spit oot greens

Wow. Good thing I persevered. This was the message I was meant to get the first time. Translation: Even though Chez Panisse thinks their vegetables are art, their preciousness would make Cher angry (people often remark on my resemblance to Cher), thus I have permission to spit the mustard greens (which are very, very bitter) oot.

This is a wonderful learning opportunity.

"Here's the polite way to get rid of something that doesn't taste good," I say to Ben.

I curl my fingers into a little horn. "Your grandpa taught me this."

I spit a mouthful of greens through the hole in my hand. "Like that."

"Really?" says Ben. He turns to my husband. "Really? 'Cause that seems kind of disgusting."

"Listen," I say. "You may not need to spit today. Or tomorrow.

But one day you'll get bones. Or marrow. Or a piece of gristle. And you'll thank me."

The waiters bring Caramelized Pear with Vin Santo ice cream and Meyer Lemon Tartlet and Pomegranate Granita. The light is amber and burnished. I feel like everybody in the room is sitting in a painting but me.

"Do you have a Tums?" I ask my husband.

"You know," my husband says, putting down his fork, "Julia and Alice were very different."

"Dental floss?"

"It's true," he says. "Julia didn't do the farm-to-table thing. She probably wondered why Alice didn't just go to the supermarket like everybody else."

He slides his glass of wine in front of me. "Drink up, love."

We are driving home when I remember what we served Julia for dessert the night she came to our house.

"Vanilla ice cream. With Grape-Nuts!" I say.

"You're *still* hungry?" asks my husband.

"No, that's what I served Julia for dessert."

He thinks about it, his fingers tapping the steering wheel. "No, it was profiteroles."

"You're wrong. I was in charge of dessert and it was Grape-Nuts ice cream. And she loved it."

"You may be right," says my husband. "I think you're right."

"What's Grape-Nuts?" asks Ben.

"A wholesome cereal made from wheat and barley," I say in a deep voice, trying to imitate Euell Gibbons. "Dawn and I used to eat them every day after school. Sprinkled on yogurt."

"They still make them, you know," says my husband.

"I should get us some."

"You should," says my husband.

"I'll go to the supermarket tomorrow."

"Well, if you're going we need orange juice, too. And eggs—not just certified organic but cage-free. And crème fraîche. And cumin—the seeds, not ground," he says. "And olive oil. But Greek olive oil, not Portuguese."

"Mmmm," I say.

He pulls into the driveway, turns to me and then sees the expression on my face.

"Hey, I have an idea. How about you go to the supermarket tomorrow and get us some Grape-Nuts?" he says.

"Good idea," I say. "They taste like wild hickory nuts."

"When have you had wild hickory nuts?"

"I haven't, but Euell Gibbons has. On the commercial. He ate cattails, too."

"I can't believe you remember that," he says.

Some of us remember dinner with famous chefs. Others of us remember cereal commercials from the seventies.

I go to Lucky's the following day. I find the Grape-Nuts and am immediately transported back in time; the box is exactly the same as it was twenty-five years ago, as is the calorie count: 200 calories for a half cup. Who eats a scant half cup of anything? No wonder I stopped buying them. Oh, what the hell. I throw them in my cart. I can do something with them for our next potluck. I'm sure there's a recipe for Grape-Nuts-encrusted meat loaf crammed somewhere in my files.

Now, what was it my husband wanted? Coriander? Ground, not the seeds?

December

A WEEK AFTER WE MOVED TO CALIFORNIA OUR DOG, BODHI, RAN AWAY. It was my fault. I left the front door wide open. I'm sure he was in shock. We were all in shock: the cloudless skies, the smiling baristas, the drivers that let you into the stream of traffic. What was wrong with these people? Surely they couldn't be this happy. Was it the six months a year of constant sunshine? Could this explain why they walked across the street so slowly, looking stunned and sometimes a little screwyouish, especially when you were trying to make a right-hand turn in your car?

We were all adjusting, but it was hardest for Bodhi. Just a few days ago his yard was fourteen acres of woods, fields and meadows. Now he was confined to a small fenced-in area and to heap insult upon insult, it seemed every other dog in California was named Bodhi. Who knew that what was a one-of-a-kind name in

Maine was the dog equivalent of Smith in the Bay Area, where if dogs weren't named Bodhi they were named something that rhymed with Bodhi, like Oatie, or Cody or Roady. That kind of thing could make anybody a little disoriented.

I made signs and posted them around the neighborhood and in town. I wrote a letter and slipped it into every mailbox on our street. I got a call the next morning.

"Is this the house that lost the dog?" said a man.

"Yes! Did you find him?" I cried.

"Do you know it's illegal to put unsolicited mail into people's private mailboxes? You could be arrested for that."

"Are you serious?" I asked.

"I'm perfectly serious," the man said.

"But we lost our dog."

"It doesn't matter. What you did is illegal," he said.

"But we just moved here and we lost our dog," I whispered.

"Maybe you should move back," said the man and hung up.

You can tell a lot about people by the command they use to tell their dogs to shit. There are many different commands in the Language of Elimination, just like in the Language of the Eskimo there are many different words for snow. Here are some examples:

> Do your business.
> Hurry up.
> Do it.
> Do it now.
> It's freaking cold out here. DO IT RIGHT NOW.
> Go potty.
> Go poo.

Do you feel like making poo?
Do your duty.

The **Do Your Business** people are usually male. Or females with Type A personalities. Which in my experience are all females over a certain age. Many females start out as **Go Poo** people and by the time they reach forty they turn into **Do Your Business** people.

The **Hurry Up** people clean the pads of the dog's feet with baby wipes before allowing them back into the house. The **Hurry Up** woman talks to herself in the car. She says: *Calm down, this is not a catastrophe. That asshole cut in front of me—it's not the end of the world. Perhaps he's having a bad day. Perhaps he just got fired from work or found out he has genital herpes.*

The **Do It, Do It Now, and It's Freaking Cold Out Here DO IT RIGHT NOW** people tend to live in the Northeast or Minnesota. They are usually jocks and they have a low percentage of body fat. They may do jumping jacks or make snow angels or twirl around while waiting for their dog to crap. They like to swat their dog on the butt after he's taken a particularly big shit.

The **Go Potty** and **Go Poo** people are without exception married with children, and usually highly educated. Often as they stand there on the sidewalk waiting for their dog to shit they are thinking about how all day long all they say is **Go Potty** and **Go Poo** and they never would have attended Princeton, Harvard, or Yale if someone had told them that ten years later they'd be talking to their dog exactly the same way they talk to their toddler. They would have saved themselves the money and the all-nighters spent in the library and just gone to some State U, where the weekends started on Wednesday nights and ended on Mondays.

The **Do You Feel Like Making Poo?** people tend to be in the counseling professions. Often they are practitioners of Reiki, massage therapists, or life coaches. If you are fortunate enough to be walking your dog at the same time as a **Do You Feel Like Making Poo?** person, you will be offered helpful suggestions such as: an empty feeling is telling me something important. They are very nice people. If you forget to bring a bag they will give you one of their bags. If you say, no, thank you, I'm allergic to plastic, they'll scoop up your dog's poo and take it home with them.

And finally, we come to the **Do Your Duty** people. I am a **Do Your Duty** person. Now, **Do Your Duty** people are sometimes mistaken for **Do Your Doodie** people. This is a big mistake, as the two types could not be more different. **Do Your Duty** people are either lawyers or doctors or the children of lawyers and doctors. **Do Your Doodie** people are clowns. No, really, I mean it—clowns, or whatever politically correct name they have for themselves now.

I am a **Do Your Duty** legacy, as my parents (both in the medical professions—my father a retired pediatrician and my mother the director of a psychiatric ward) used **Do Your Duty** with great success on our childhood dog, Greta. You know you are a **Do Your Duty** legacy if one of your memories is of your mother asking you if you had a BM today.

I am not proud to be a **Do Your Duty** person, I find the phrase a little cold and Third Reichish, but you can't help the elimination phrase that's been passed down to you. If I could, I'd make a new category and become a **How About You Do It on the $3,000 Rug** person.

Ben was only two when Bodhi ran away, so he doesn't remember how empty the house was without him or how mad my husband was at me for leaving the front door open. It was a sign that we never should have made the move across the country to a place where we had no family or friends. We should have left Bodhi in Maine with my sister Sara, where he could have lived his life being the one-of-a-kind dog he really was. But we were selfish. We could not imagine our new life without Bodhi in it.

We were lucky. A doctor found Bodhi and took him to his house. Then this kind doctor posted notices at all the pounds and area vets even though he'd instantly fallen in love with Bodhi and decided he would keep him if nobody came to claim him.

It was a shimmering Northern California day when we got Bodhi back. We were so grateful that we gave the doctor a wad of cash and a package of Fudge Stripe Cookies (Ben's contribution), neither of which he accepted. He left quickly. He had tears in his eyes. I think Bodhi would have had a fine life with this man, a different life to be sure, but a fine, happy life, but I can't think too much about that because you could drive yourself crazy thinking about all the lives you almost lived but didn't.

It's seven years later, and I am watching Bodhi poop on my antique kilim rug because he's too lame and incontinent to make it outside anymore. I will never have to say **Do Your Duty** again. In fact, I am no longer in charge of his doodie. Neither, it appears, is he.

I get the roll of paper towels and the spray bottle of 409.

"Bad boy," I say, but I don't mean it. His decline is heartbreaking. Soon we will have to do something about it.

After we found Bodhi, I suggested to my husband that we rename him. Life might be easier for him if he had more of a stand-out name. Something to make him feel special again. Something retro, a name that hadn't yet resurfaced and become fashionable—like Spot.

"Spot?" said my husband.

"Yes. Nobody in the Bay Area would name their dog Spot," I say. "Dogs in Northern California are named after gods and operas and planets. You have Hera and Puccini and Saturn, but no Spot."

"Barky," said Ben.

"That would be perfect," I said, "if only he barked."

Bodhi never barked, not even when robbers backed their van up to our house and carted nearly everything away, including all my husband's suits and Ben's globe (which explains why to this day he thinks Florida is a continent).

"How about Bodhi spelled Bodi?" said my husband.

"Like Patrick Swayze in that surf movie?" I said.

"I think this is a terrible idea. You can't just change somebody's name," said my husband.

"Even if they're going through a midlife crisis?"

"Dogs don't go through a midlife crisis."

"Of course they do. Bodhi's seven—that's forty-nine in people years. That's why he ran away. He needs a new name. He needs to shake things up. He's wondering what he's going to do with the rest of his life."

"I'll tell you what he's going to do with the rest of his life. Eat, sleep, shit, drool, look at us wistfully, and catch balls. The same thing he did with the first part of his life."

I was getting nowhere. I decided to speak in a language my husband could understand: "Bodhi's running away was his 108-day Outward Bound course. His ascent on Mount McKinley. He's looking for a new identity. He wants to reinvent himself."

This was a bit of flattery. My husband did a 108-day Outward Bound course and made an ascent on Mount McKinley.

"Didn't you have a secret name on the OB course? Like Trail-feather or Mongo?" I asked.

My husband glared at me. "Have you been reading my journal?"

At that time we'd been together for eight years. Did he really think I was still reading his journal?

I couldn't get anyone to agree with me to change Bodhi's name so I changed it secretly. When my family was around I called him Bodhi, but when I was alone in the house I called him Spot. Bodhi had no idea I was talking to him, but calling him Spot made me unduly happy, as though I'd found a way to cheat time. I felt like a child again, like he and I were living inside the Dick and Jane books I read when I was a kid. This was a world where nothing bad ever happened, where dogs stayed puppies forever, where nobody became incontinent or had any problems getting up off the floor.

I ran away from home once when I was eleven. Why? Well, it could have been for any number of reasons. I was wrongly accused of eating more than my share of the Nilla Wafers. I was wrongly accused of eating an entire one-pound package of Twizzlers. I was rightly accused of eating six bowls of tapioca.

"I'm going to run away," I told my mother.

"Need any help packing?" she asked.

I remember the feeling of freedom as I walked down the street. It was summer. The air smelled of tar and faintly of the sea. I had a secret name for myself. Whenever I endured some hardship, something that would literally bring me to my knees, like being forced to muck out the horse's stall or weed rhubarb, I became Sara Crewe of *A Little Princess*. It was the orphan Sara who was running away, in search of her savior who unbeknownst to her was living in the building across the street from her mouse-infested garret.

"Where do you think you're going?" said my father, pulling up behind me in the Plymouth Valiant.

Dawn was in the front seat sucking on a Charms Blow Pop that she had saved from the previous Sunday's candy day. She was a saver and I was a spender. It was so annoying.

I kept running away. They kept creeping behind me in the Valiant, cramping my style. Sammy Johns's "Chevy Van" was playing on the radio, and despite the dire situation I perked up. Every fifth-grade girl I knew loved that song (although none of us knew what it was really about). I began singing along.

I gave a girl a ride in my wagon
She crawled in and took control
She was tired 'cause her mind was a-draggin'
I said, get some sleep and dream of rock and roll

'Cause like a princess she was layin' there
Moonlight dancin' off her hair
She woke up and took me by the hand
We made love in my Chevy van
And that's all right with me.

I had never seen a Chevy van but I really wanted to lie in the back of one. Thinking about it made me all tingly.

"You should get in the car," warned Dawn.

"Get the hell in the car," shouted my father, stabbing his fingers at the radio dial, trying to turn it off.

I got in the car and started sobbing. The kind of sobbing that Sara Crewe must have done when she found out her father's friend, Mr. Carmichael, had been looking for her the whole time she had been emptying chamberpots and befriending mice.

The next day my father took me to Woolworth's. He let me buy all the candy I wanted, even though it wasn't Sunday. I bought fudge and peanut brittle and a box of Mike and Ike's for my mother. I bought nothing for my sisters.

After I was done stuffing my face he asked me why I had run away.

"I want to live somewhere different," I told him.

"Where?"

"Somewhere where there aren't so many antiques," I said.

We lived in a 1700s colonial that my parents had painstakingly restored and decorated with period pieces. We watched TV on uncomfortable wooden settees. We slept on horsehair mattresses and every Christmas we stuck cloves into oranges to make pomanders.

"One day you'll appreciate the antiques," said my father.

"I doubt that," I said.

On the way home I looked out the window and whispered the truth. "I wish I was an only child."

"You shouldn't say things like that," said my father.

"You could send me to boarding school," I said.

All the girls in the books that I read went to boarding school. It sounded romantic and glamorous.

"You would miss your sisters," he said, after a pause.

"No, I would not."

"You don't think so, but you would."

When my father was five his mother died, and he was sent away to boarding school, but he wouldn't tell me that for another ten years. It would take another ten years and a child of my own for me to grasp the magnitude of this fact.

My father reached across the seat, picked up my hand and held it. He was not a hand-holder and he didn't hold my hand for very long, but it was enough.

When we got home I gave my mother the box of Mike and Ike's.

"That's very thoughtful of you," she said.

I went up to my room. Through the open window I could hear my sisters playing outside: the pounding of their feet on the lawn as they did round-offs and back flips; the soft thrum of their voices as they lay in the grass and stared up at the sky.

I was very full from all the fudge and peanut brittle. Right before dinner my mother came upstairs and rapped on the frame of the bedroom door.

"I would have found you," she said. "I wouldn't have let you go. You know that, don't you?"

I gave a little groan. "My stomach hurts."

"I'm sure it does," she said. "Have you had a BM today?"

There have been times in my life when I envied Bodhi. The day we brought Ben home from the hospital, for instance, and he cried for six hours without stopping until I screamed, "What the fuck have we done!" at my husband. Bodhi heaved a big I-told-you-having-this-baby-was-a-bad-idea sigh and went upstairs and stayed upstairs until Ben turned two.

Things I do not envy about Bodhi: he has had to eat the same thing day in and day out for thirteen years; he has never had dinner at Dona Tomas; he has no idea that we're plotting his death.

We've arranged to have him euthanized at home. Our friends who have been through this tell us this is the humane thing to do, but it feels like we've paid a thug to come in and shoot him in the head. We've had many conversations with the vet. The vet is not a thug. He's gentle and patient and we keep telling him the same things over and over again.

He can't make it up the stairs anymore. *But we'll carry him.*

He can't make it outside. *But we'll pull him in the wagon.*

He's confined to one room. *But we live in a one-room shanty.*

And then one day when we tell the vet he can't make it up the stairs anymore for the umpteenth time the vet says, *How about I come next Sunday?*

How does one go about the days burdened with this terrible knowledge?

I try to act perfectly normal around Bodhi. I don't want him to suspect anything is wrong. He's a typical Lab: he parses everything with his heart. If I do anything out of the ordinary he will know something's up. So I say what I have always said. I say "bad boy," when he pees on the hardwood floor. I say "yuck" when I wipe the twin strands of drool off his muzzle. But in my mind I am imagining him on his best day. A svelte one hundred pounds, leaping off a rock into the middle of the St. George River in Maine. Gobbling down an entire cooked turkey that we had left on the counter to cool.

I must have a very strange look on my face when I'm summoning up these memories, a kind of twisted grin because Bodhi gives his worried-for-the-people-I-love murmur. *Erm, Erm,* he says, trying to comfort me.

"No, it's all right," I say, trying to focus on him flying through the air, enjoying the perfectly browned turkey breast. But right after he leaped off that rock he climbed back up another one and in doing so tore his Achilles tendon.

There was lots of blood. We raced him to the vet.

And that turkey he ate was for our Thanksgiving dinner, which was put on hold because (A) we no longer had a turkey and (B) our dog had eaten an entire turkey!

There was lots of vomit. We raced him to the vet.

We call our old friend the vet. What do we do? How do we prepare Bodhi? Really we are asking what do *we* do? How do *we* prepare ourselves?

The vet knows this, of course, and his answer for both of us is treats. Treats apparently distract the dog from the fact he is about to be given an injection and die. Treats will distract us too, from the fact that we are horrible people who set up the appointment where our beloved dog will be given an injection and die.

I go to the pet store. I get the storeroom guy to help me put Bodhi in a carriage and then I wheel him through the aisles. He holds his head erect like Henry the VIII. Anything he shows the least amount of interest in I buy: Pup-Peroni, pig's ears, Baa-Baa-Q's and liver biscotti. Bodhi is drooling all over the carriage in anticipation, but I'm sure they're used to that kind of thing. We are in a pet store, after all, and we are in California, where people have birthday parties for their dogs and take them on day trips to Napa where they drink special doggie wine and do doga. I race past the toy and ball aisle. We are on the other side of toys. We are also on the other side of treats supplemented with omega-3's and wheatgrass. We are *not*, however, on the other side of Woofy Pop. I toss a package into the carriage.

"Wow, lucky dog," says the cashier, when she sees all the loot. "What's the occasion?"

"Last supper," I say under my breath.

"Does he always drool like that?" she asks.

"Labs drool," I tell her.

"Maybe you should get him checked. Take him to the vet."

"That's a very good idea," I say.

I make a quick stop at the bakery and get some treats for us— some Christmas tree cookies. This will be the first Christmas Ben has ever had without Bodhi.

Ben knows that Bodhi's been steadily declining and is ninety-four in people years, the same age as his great-grandmother, and that he may go suddenly at any time, but we haven't told him we've paid someone to come to the house and finish him off. Our plan is to send Ben on a playdate and when he comes home tell him Bodhi passed away while he was busy playing Star Wars Lego Wii. This is probably not the right thing to do; perhaps he'll be scarred for life, but we don't think he'll be able to bear the premeditated part of it all. I'm pretty sure he's going to grow up and become a **Do You Feel Like Making Poo?** person. If he were a **Do Your Business** person we'd tell him the truth. Thank God, he's not.

We are given lots of advice from well-meaning friends: make Bodhi's passing a ritual, play music, light candles, write something and read it out loud. One friend tells me to clear the house of the dog's things beforehand so you won't be triggered every time you walk past his dog bed or empty water bowl. This last suggestion makes the most sense to me (I'm thinking of Ben), but I can't bring myself to do much of anything but sit there in a chair while waiting for the vet to arrive. I begin crying as soon as the doorbell rings.

Bodhi is lying in the hallway sleeping off last night's binge but he wakes at the sound of the doorbell. He lifts his head and looks at me. I am trapped in his look, just as he is trapped in his body. It's the look my father gave me in the car, when I was running away. It's the look that was on my face the first time I saw my husband walk into a room. It's the look Ben gave me this morning when we insisted that he pet Bodhi one more time before he went on his playdate.

The vet has brought paperwork and a nurse.

The vet says you are doing the right thing.

The vet says this is the last great act of love.

My husband carries Bodhi from the hallway into the dining room and places him gently on a blanket. We feed him more treats and the vet gives him the first injection. Within a few seconds he stops eating from my hand and becomes very, very still, but he isn't dead yet.

I won't bore you with what we say. We say what every person says when somebody they love is dying.

The vet gives him the second injection.

Go home, Spot, I whisper in Bodhi's ear.

The nurse and the doctor carry him away, wrapped in the blanket. After they have driven off, I open the front door and I leave the front door open all day long.

January

I HAVE ONLY ONE NEW YEAR'S RESOLUTION, TO *AGE GRACEFULLY*, WHICH IS really code for lose ten pounds because every woman knows this is the secret to aging gracefully. It doesn't matter how old you are if you still look good in a pair of yoga pants. Size 6 = power, happiness and joy. Size 10 = much less power, happiness and joy. I hate that this is true.

The best I can hope for is to put on a pair of yoga pants and look okay as long as I wear a longish shirt over the yoga pants. My friend Kerri, who manages a boutique, tells me the shirt I'm talking about is called a tunic and lucky for me tunics have made a comeback, but I can't bring myself to buy one. They make me think of Bea Arthur and Maude, so instead I wear my husband's Van Halen World Tour T-shirt inside out.

I thought that caring less about how I looked would be one of the benefits of getting older, much in the same way I am currently deluding myself into thinking that by the time Ben leaves for college, higher education will be free. Caring less about how I look is certainly an option, but a painful one because when I care less so does everybody else and then I am mistaken for a sixty-year-old. Take for instance what happened a few years ago when my sister Sara came to visit.

Sara is eight years younger than I am. She had a completely different childhood than mine. Once we all left for college, she became an only child. She had it easy—her cross to bear was being too popular. How nice it must have been for my parents to have a daughter whom everybody adored. I'm sure it was the life they had always dreamed of: one perfect child who loved Pop Rocks, Sean Cassidy and the cello.

Sara tells me my parents used to introduce her by saying, "And here's our Sara."

It's the "our" that kills me. When my parents introduced the three of us older girls it went something like "This is Rebecca; she's taking advanced calculus. Oh, yes, and those two whacking each other over the head with their Sasha dolls are the twins."

You can't hold Sara's charm against her. She emanates light. I would emanate light, too, if my name didn't mean darkness. I have always meant to ask my parents what's with naming Dawn and me after musical acts of the seventies and giving our sisters classic names out of the Bible? I mean why didn't they go all the way and just name us after fashions popular at the time, like Maxi and Hot Pants?

Ben was only three the time Sara came to visit us in California, and he was starstruck every time she spoke to him or looked his way. I figured he was confused because Sara and I looked so much alike. Was she his mother or his aunt?

Sara wore no makeup. Nor did she need any. She was so stunning and fresh-faced that I became convinced I could pull off the same look. I put my mascara away. I eschewed lipstick for Vaseline and off we went for a walk around the block.

Soon we ran into a woman and her husband.

"Oh, my God," the woman squealed. "You two look so much alike!"

I beamed and hooked my arm in Sara's.

"Your daughter is beautiful," gushed the woman to me.

"Have you thought about where you want to go to college yet?" she said to Sara.

Her husband saw the stricken look on my face and pinched his wife's elbow discreetly. "I don't think they're mother and daughter," he whispered.

"But they look so much alike!" said the woman.

"That's because we're sisters," said Sara.

"Honey, we should go," said the husband.

"But you look so young," said the woman to Sara. "You could be in high school."

"I'm thirty. In order for her to be my mother she would have had to have given birth to me when she was eight," said Sara, trying to prop me up.

I was so devastated I would have fallen to my knees in the middle of the street had Sara not been holding on to me. The weird thing was I didn't feel like my mother. I actually felt like my father. This was worse than being mistaken for my mother, as my father was nearly seventy.

"I wasn't saying she looks old. It's just that you look so young," repeated the woman to Sara, flashing me a dirty look as if it was my fault she had been duped.

I don't want to dupe anyone. I don't want to be one of those women who from the back looks twenty but from the front looks like Jessica Tandy. At the same time, I want to look good for my age but not so good that people wonder which procedures I've had done. In short I want to look like the best version of my real self. I want to be at peace with the fact that I am forty-four and this is what forty-four looks like and it looks pretty good!

I do a bang-up job of feeling this way until I make the mistake of picking up *More* magazine, which tells me "this is what forty-four looks like" and it doesn't look anything like me. Forty-four in *More* looks like twenty-two and I'm back to square one, trying to lose ten pounds and wondering how in God's name anyone ages gracefully.

I never thought it would happen to me. When you're fifteen and twenty and twenty-five and thirty-five and you look younger than you are, you think this will always be the case. You'll never look your age. Until one day you do. But you don't quite get it. You keep forgetting. You keep walking around thinking you're passing for thirty until one day it hits you that unless you put a great deal of effort into it, unless you wear lipstick and mascara and exercise seven days a week you are for all intents and purposes invisible. People look past you and over and around you and above you, except the women your age, who are staring right at you, taking in your shoes and your hair and your face and your clothes and wondering, *God, I hope I don't look as bad as she does. And what's with the husband's T-shirt? Why doesn't she wear one of those cute new tunics that are in style?*

My friends and I search for our lost selves everywhere. We look in the backs of teaspoons, in the elevator doors right before they close, in the mirrors above the produce in the grocery store and in the lyrics of the songs that played at our weddings. Where is that plucky girl, that lustful teenager, that optimistic young woman, that tenderhearted young mother? Where have they all gone?

Occasionally, if we are lucky, we catch a glimpse of the woman we are becoming. This woman is our future; she is the one who has been aging gracefully inside of us. She is more than her body. She is more than her face. She is, as James Salter wrote, a woman whose "dreams still cling to her . . . related to long-necked creatures, ruminants, abandoned saints."

I love these lines. I love this woman. My deepest hope is to track her down and convince her to move into the apartment that houses my soul before I die. I would do anything to get her to inhabit me. I would even lie and tell her I have a three-bedroom with a four-bridge view instead of the threadbare studio where my neglected soul currently dwells.

I should go to church. Find a religion. Meditate. Hike every day. Get a new dog. Take magnesium. Drink carrot juice. And above all, stop looking in the mirror. Because when I do I notice the ridge. The ridge on my head that I really, really should do something about.

Do you know about Japanese Thermal Straightening? If your hair is straight, chances are you have no idea what I am talking about. But if you are like me, half Indian and half Armenian, someone who has fought her thick, curly hair all her life, you know *exactly* what I am talking about and you know that this procedure is prohibitively expensive (to the tune of $600) and addictive. Once you start Japanese Thermal Straightening your hair it's very hard to stop.

What is this ridge? It's the three inches of new growth on the top of my head. The Japanese Thermal Straightening grows out like a perm, only in reverse. Instead of straight on top and curly on the ends, my hair is curly on top and straight on the ends. Take my word for it when I tell you this ridge makes it difficult to continue passing as a naturally straight-haired woman (especially when it rains, is humid, is windy, the sun shines, somebody coughs or there is any sort of a breeze), and that is the whole point of doing Japanese Thermal Straightening. *Passing.*

If you are saying to yourself *What's wrong with you, I would love to have a head of curls like yours,* then you obviously have straight hair. The rest of you, calm down. I am not about to spend $600 getting my hair straightened, which is why I am on my way to Chinatown, where I can get it done for $125 with tip. As I'm walking past St. Mary's Square, I call my sister Rebecca, who lives in New York City and who is probably at this moment sitting in some hair salon getting her hair straightened, too. We are on the same hair-straightening cycle, much like we used to get our periods at the same time when we were teenagers.

"I'm on my way to get my hair straightened," I tell her.

"I just got mine done," she says. "My hairdresser used to work for Sally Hershberger."

She always tells me this.

"Yes, but mine only costs $100."

I always lower the price.

"That is so unfair," she says. "Maybe I should fly to California to get my hair straightened. Even with the flight it'd be cheaper. Is your hair falling out yet?"

Rebecca and I used to be equals on the fashion front. This was twenty years ago when she was at Smith College and I was at Emerson College and we both weighed 120 pounds. Then she moved to Tribeca. Now she weighs 105 pounds and is a lawyer at the Metropolitan Museum of Art. I won't tell you what I weigh except to say it's slightly more than 120 pounds.

"I've got to go. I'm here," I say.

"What's the name of the salon?" asks Rebecca.

I look up at the sign. I've never noticed the name of the salon. I just know the phone number and street.

"Express Hair Salon, with an X," I say. "Like 'X-Press.' "

More silence in which Rebecca thinks *Are you fucking kidding me* and some more silence in which I am thinking but not saying the same thing.

"The lady just saw me. She's looking at me through the window. She's beckoning me in," I say.

"She remembers you?" says Rebecca.

They absolutely remember me. I have been coming every six months for the last seven years.

Julie sits me in a chair.

"Hello, hello," she says. "You have an appointment?"

"Nine," I tell her.

"You're smart to come early."

We laugh. We joke. She brings me a nice cup of tea. Then she parts my hair, lifting up the layers, peering underneath, and says, "Your hair is very, very frizzy."

"Not so frizzy," I say.

"Frizziest hair I ever saw. You have a nice tan, though," she says.

She's trying to figure out my ethnicity. She's wondering if I'm African American. Japanese Thermal Straightening does not work on African American hair.

"Thank you," I say, which is easier than saying it's not a tan.

You can have many conversations at one time at the beauty parlor. Besides race and class we are also talking about money.

"Your hair is very resistant," she says. "Especially here in the back."

In the back where I can't see and I'll just have to take her word for it.

"I'll have to do it two times," she says. "Two applications. What time do you have to be home?"

"Three. I have to pick up my son from school."

"No problem, we'll have you out by three."

Yes, here is my secret shame—the lengths to which I will go to look unlike my true self. I will be sitting in this chair for the NEXT SIX HOURS.

"How much?" I ask.

"$150. We only take cash. The ATM is across the street."

It's gone up twenty-five-dollars but it's still a deal.

"You go to a fancy salon in Union Square, you'll pay $500, $600," says Julie.

"That can't be right!" I say, as if this is news to me. I'm afraid she's about to raise the price. "Who could afford that?"

Metamorphosis is not a linear process. At least for me it's not. It's dull and it's boring and it takes many, many years. It consists of my teaching myself the same lesson over and over again until I finally get it right.

The first couple of hours are fun. I feel a little manic, but pleasurably manic, as if it's the night before I'm traveling to Paris and I have to get up at three in the morning to leave for the airport. I think about popping an Ativan. Instead I crack open my six-hundred-page novel. When I look up, it's noon and the Chinatown streets are bustling. I can smell shrimp dumplings and kung pao chicken but I can't leave and partake of any of these delicious treats because my head is swathed in a ball of Saran Wrap. I eat an entire bag of ginger chews and the hours slowly tick by.

At two I say to Julie, "I have to pick up my son. Across the Bay. In Oakland."

At two thirty I say, "I have to leave *now.*" They are still flat-ironing my hair.

At three I am nearly in tears, frantically calling Robin to ask if she'll pick Ben up from school along with her daughter, Sadie.

"What are you doing?" Robin asks. "Something fun and indulgent, I hope."

"I'm getting my hair done," I say.

"Lucky you," she says. "Take your time and have fun!"

Finally I'm finished.

"You know the rules," says Julie. "No washing for four days. Do not get your hair wet. Do not sweat. I suggest you sleep on your back. Do not go out in the wind. No barrettes, no bobby pins, no headbands, not even tucking your hair behind your ears."

Or else I will walk around for the next six months with an ear-shaped indentation in my hair. Oh, well, at least the ridge is gone and my hair is straight. So straight my features look distorted. I tug at the roots, trying to get some volume.

"Don't do that," says Julie. "You'll ruin it."

She smears her hands with silicone gel and plasters my hair back to my head.

"There—straight."

"It's really, really straight," I say.

"You husband will love it," she says, whipping off the cape.

This wasn't the first time I tried to make myself into somebody I wasn't.

When I was eleven I fell in love with Tatum O'Neal. Well, maybe it wasn't so much love as it was infatuation. I wanted to be her and if I couldn't *be* her . . .

"Maybe I could just move in with Tatum and Ryan," I said to my mother.

I was trying to prepare her, you see. I had written to Tatum a few weeks earlier suggesting that very thing. That I could be a sort of super-duper pen pal who would not only write to her every day but was also available to come live with her in her bedroom. Kind of like a twin, I suggested.

"That's nice," said my mother. "Who's Ryan? Her boyfriend?"

"Ryan O'Neal. Her father? *Love Story?* You know, never having to say you're sorry?" I said.

"Oh, I loved that movie." She smiled a soft private smile as if all the secrets of the world were lodged in the corners of her mouth. It made me feel terribly left out.

"But how would I get to California?" I asked.

"Don't worry," my mother said. "If the O'Neals want to adopt you, your father and I can cover the cost of the plane ticket."

But it wasn't Tatum I wanted to be. I really wanted to be Addie Loggins, the character she played in *Paper Moon.* Was there ever a more kick-ass girl? Cigar-smoking, undershirt-wearing, swindling-widows-out-of-their-last-dime Addie Loggins?

There was only one small problem. There was nobody in America who looked less like Addie Loggins than me. But I would fix that. I showed my Uncle Tommy, who was a hairdresser, a picture of Tatum. She was dressed in a tuxedo, holding the Oscar.

"Like this," I told him.

"But she's a blonde," he said, sweeping my long hair up into a ponytail. "And her hair is straight and fine. It won't come out like that."

"Just do it," I said.

"You look like a carp," Uncle Tommy said sadly when he was done, looking with dismay at my black curls, like hundreds of apostrophes scattered on the linoleum. He was right. I did look like I had jumped species; my head was too big for my body now. I made a noise that was something between a squeal and a squeak.

"I think she looks nice," my mother said, resting her hands on my shoulders.

She tried to fluff up my hair but had little success, as it was a quarter of an inch long. That's how short Uncle Tommy had to go to get it straight.

"You look like Cher. Doesn't everybody always say that to you? That you look like Cher?" my mother reminded me.

"She looked like Cher half an hour ago. Now she looks like she has a bad case of lice," said my father, grimacing. This would reflect badly on him, the daughter of the town's pediatrician with nits.

About six months later a large manila envelope came in the mail. When I saw it was postmarked California I knew exactly what it was—Tatum had finally written back! Nobody had believed she would, but I never gave up. Instead I spent countless hours fantasizing about my new life in California. Tatum's bedroom would have a shag carpet and beanbag chairs. We would wear denim wraparound skirts, peasant blouses and white go-go boots. There would be some hardships, of course. I would have to develop a taste for papaya, as Californians consumed great quantities of the sticky orange fruit—that's how they stayed so svelte. Most of my daydreams centered on me getting off the plane and stepping onto the tarmac where Tatum and Ryan waited for me.

"We look so much alike. We could be twins," Tatum would say.

Ryan would throw his arms around us both. "Let's go to Hollywood and Vine and grab a bite."

I tore open the envelope. Inside were three glossies of Tatum O'Neal and she had autographed each one with a black Magic Marker. The first was a photograph of her as Addie Loggins, wearing that funny little hat. The second was of Tatum holding a bat in *Bad News Bears*. And the third was a smaller snapshot of Tatum sitting on Ryan's lap. It said: For Melanie, XOXO, Tatum.

It made me sad, that last picture. In my house eleven-year-olds didn't sit on their father's lap.

"I'm very sorry I lost faith," said my mother.

"That's okay," I said.

I could afford to forgive my mother because my status had changed. I had gone from lowly twin with horrible haircut and deluded fantasies to favorite daughter who, due to pluck and persistence, was now in regular correspondence with famous child actor.

Buoyed by the photographs, which made me a celebrity for about a week, I continued to write to Tatum for a year, first suggesting, then pleading, then begging for her to write back to me. But I never got any response.

I stopped making Uncle Tommy cut my hair, or maybe my mother wisely began taking me to somebody I wasn't related to. My father was never my pediatrician. Why would my uncle be my hairdresser? Hair is just as much about life and death and transformation as height percentiles and having to deliver to somebody the very bad news that they are going to have to get a shot today.

It's dinnertime by the time I make it back to Oakland. Despite Julie's dire warnings to not put anything on my head, I am now wearing a cloche so Robin won't see my straighter-than-straight hair. I look like Ali McGraw in *Love Story*—at least that's what I tell myself. Four days from now when I can wash my hair and put product in it, I'll look normal. Until then I won't leave the house.

"What's up with the hat? It's seventy degrees out," says Robin.

"Brr," I say.

Robin has beautiful Eileen Fisher hair. Do you know what I'm talking about? The Eileen Fisher models with the gray hair? But it's to-die-for gray hair. By this I mean straight and swingy and blunt cut and it makes you look so young and hip. It's a fabulous look, one that will never be mine.

Ben and Robin's daughter, Sadie, stampede into the room.

"Why are you wearing a hat indoors?" says Ben.

"Because lots of people wear hats indoors in California," I say.

This is true and this is a lie. Lots of people who are twenty-four, not forty-four, wear their hats indoors.

"We're not allowed to wear hats in school," says Ben.

Sadie nods in agreement.

"Go away," says Robin to the kids.

"Now, how bad is it?" she says to me.

"You don't want to know."

"Just show me. You can't screw up straight hair," says Robin.

Robin has no idea I've been faking it all these years.

"Yes, you can," I say.

"Well, you're making it worse, wearing that hat. Now you'll have hat head on top of a bad haircut. Go home, wash it, style it yourself," says Robin. "You'll feel better."

"Excellent idea," I say, thinking of the next four days I'll spend hiding in the house.

After I get home and stick dinner in the oven, Ben and I walk up the street to our secret place—a tree stump that has an unbelievable view of the Pacific. He brings a Moleskine notebook so he can sketch things: leaves, the bay, poison oak. I bring a mug of wine so I can forget things: the fact that Tatum O'Neal never wrote back to me but still I went on loving her and to this day love her still.

Ben decides he wants to sketch me. I am not in the mood to be sketched, but perhaps it will put me in a better mood.

It does not:

"Where's my hat? You didn't draw my hat."

"I drew what was underneath your hat."

"Does my hairline really look that?"

"You have a big forehead," he says.

"Yes, but has it gotten bigger? Since you've known me?"

What I'm asking him is *Has my hairline receded?* The Japanese Thermal Straightening has definitely thinned my hair out.

Ben sighs, which means yes, but I'm not stupid enough to say so. He has learned this particular sigh from his dad.

"This is a ridiculous hat," I say.

"It's a girl's hat," he says, thinking I'm about to suggest that he wear it.

"It's called a cloche," I say.

I take off the hat.

"Wow, your hair's straight," he says.

"Not that straight," I say.

"No, it's really straight. Like a—like a—I can't think of what it's like," he says.

It's windy and my hair begins to whip around my face. Just like that, six hours, $150 gone. I feel liberated and then I panic. I slap the hat back on my head again.

"I know. Your hair is like a wall!" he cries.

"No, it's not," I huff.

"It is. It's like two walls hanging down from your face."

I take the hat off again.

A few summers ago my mother and I had a conversation. We were talking about what happens after you die. I told her that now that I was a mother I wanted to believe in heaven. I *needed* to believe in heaven. She told me that at sixty-seven she no longer believed in heaven, but she finally understood why we were here.

My mother runs a psychiatric ward. Daily, she walks the borders between what's seen and unseen. She is the kind of person you would want to have around in an emergency: clear-thinking, unafraid and compassionate. She is not, however, touchy-feely. She is not one of those mothers who send out Christmas letters highlighting their daughters' accomplishments. She is a Rhode Islander. She says "bah" for *bar* and knows how to get every bit of meat out of a lobster, and she eats all the lobster, including the green and red gunk. What I'm trying to say is she's the real thing.

On that balmy August night, she told me the reason she was here was to have children. To do her part in ensuring the human race went on. And that was it. When she died her family would remember her and she would live on in their memories for seventy years at most, and then she would be forgotten. She would become one of the ninety billion people on this planet that had lived and died before her. The end.

I thought this was one of the most romantic and beautiful things I had ever heard my mother say. It didn't seem futile to me, her way of thinking. It was what you would come to after a lifetime of never taking the easy way out; never wishing you were somebody else; never trying to pass for something you were not.

At forty-four, I feel the current of that river pulling at me. I am one of six and a half billion people currently taking their turn at being alive on this planet. One of billions trying to make sense of their lives, their heartbreaks, their regrets, their greatest loves, their bad knees, and their beloved children sitting in front of them who will one day be part of the billions who have come before and have long since been forgotten.

This is unfathomable. And it's the truest thing I know.

Down below us San Francisco is buried in a fog so thick you wouldn't even know a city was there. But here on this hillside the stars are coming out and the breeze smells of granite and hamburgers.

"Home," I say to Ben.

He tucks his notebook into his pocket and slips his hand in mine.

February

TWO THINGS I KNOW FOR SURE BUT WON'T TELL MY SON AT THE PRESENT moment because I don't want to rub it in are that once you become an adult you hardly ever cry or vomit. I won't tell him this because right now he is doing both. Crying, because even though it's two months after our dog died, he feels even more bereft than he did right after he received the news, and vomiting because he's got the flu. The good thing about being nine is you can puke into a bucket and not get any of it on the rug. The bad thing is you still occasionally puke out of your nose.

"You won't vomit out of your nose when you're an adult," I tell him.

"Yeah, right," he says, wiping his nose.

"I'm not kidding. Something closes. Some passageway that connects your nose to your mouth."

I'm making this up. How do I know why you stop vomiting out of your nose once you become an adult?

"Then how do you breathe?" he asks. "If the passageway closes up?"

"You hardly breathe at all when you're an adult."

I am not making that up.

We lie on the couch together and watch *Avatar*. That makes him feel better but it makes me feel worse. There are so many things I have to do right now, like get earthquake insurance and learn to knit. I am always in a hurry. The other day when I was in San Francisco some guy told me I was walking too fast.

"Walking that fast should be against the law," he said.

He got my attention. The laws in San Francisco were completely different than those in any other American city. For all I knew it *was* illegal to walk too fast in the City by the Bay.

"L'Arte del vivere con lentezza," he continued. "The Art of Living Slowly."

"Excuse me, but what language are you speaking?"

"Italian."

"Well, then. *Prego*," I said proudly.

I had recently learned that *prego* means thank you, not pregnant. I've been dying for an opportunity to use it in everyday conversation.

"Speed-walking is not good for you," he said.

"Are you okay?" I asked him.

He-was-speaking-very-slow-ly. I wanted to wave my hand at him to speed him up but I thought this would be rude. I did, however, wave my hand at him in my imagination and a little smile crept across my face.

"See, you are happier already," he said.

He handed me a piece of paper.

Bruno's Slowmandments, I read at the top.

"Bruno?" I asked.

"No, I am just a follower. Read number seven, please," he said.

I scanned the page: Avoid being so busy and full of work that you don't have time for yourself and the delight of thinking about nothing. Also, avoid using contractions (this is scribbled in pencil).

I handed the piece of paper back to him, saying, "Thanks, but no. This isn't my kind of thing."

"Yes, I can see that. That is why I stopped you," he said pleasantly.

"I think you have mistaken me for a native Californian," I said.

"I do not think so," he said.

"I'm from Rhode Island."

He looked bewildered.

"Rhode Island is right next door to New York, assuming you don't count Connecticut. We have very similar accents; I say things like *tawk* and *dawg* and *cawfee* and *cawl* for talk and dog and coffee and call and the point is we don't do anything slowly. We're incapable of it."

Delight in thinking about nothing? Please. I didn't even take baths.

He thrust a clipboard at me. "Would you sign this? We are trying to make San Francisco an official Slow City."

The thought of San Francisco being slower than it already was—was terrifying. People cross the streets so slowly here it's an act of aggression. In New York City people hustle. I was in a cab once that purposely hit a man who jaywalked. The driver actually sped up in order to hit him. I learned my lesson. You run or you die.

"Sorry, but no," I said.

"You don't want to live a better life?"

I shook my head. Slowly.

He shrugged and walked away. I watched him stop a woman on a bike. Within a few minutes they were chatting like old friends. She opened her fanny pack and pulled out two Odwalla bars and they sat down on the grass. Their heads bowed together, they began reading the Slowmandments. It was noon. They would be there until dusk.

"I'll think about it," I shouted to the man, feeling abandoned and a little sad.

Why couldn't I be more like the woman on the bike? Trusting. Curious. Willing to share her snacks.

I'll be right back," I say to Ben.

"No." He grabs my arm with desperation. "What if I have to throw up again?"

I point to the bucket. "I-just-have-to-go-to-the-bathroom."

I try and speak like the Slow Living guy, haltingly and without contractions. I have to admit it feels good. My anxiety at being trapped in the house with a sick kid dials down a few notches.

"When are we going to get a new dog?" says Ben.

And then it shoots up again.

Ben asks me this at least once a week. My standard line is "It wouldn't be fair to Bodhi if we got another dog so soon," but I know this line will only be good for a few months and then I'll have to come up with another one. The truth is that as much as I miss Bodhi I don't want to get another dog. I like the freedom: nobody doing his duty on my carpets; no more kennels, no vacuuming the dog hair.

We have a Bodhi shrine. It's a marvelous shrine. It's like having Bodhi without the Bodhi. For a while it was under our dining room table. It consisted of his dog bed strewn with twenty pounds of dog food. Ben spent a lot of time under the table, lying next to the dog bed, sifting the dog food through his fingers, and I spent a lot of time praying the dog food wouldn't attract mice. Just yesterday we had to relocate the shrine because we had ants, we had ants, we had ants. It's a much cozier shrine now. There is a box containing Bodhi's ashes, a photograph of him in a meadow in Maine, and a farewell note saying:

> I love you so much and I miss you, too. I hope you are
> having a good time in heaven.
> Love,
> Ben, your beloved trainer

Yes, I'm not proud of it, but under a great deal of pressure I invented a new heaven. A heaven just for dogs where all they do all day long is run and chase squirrels and eat Woofy Pop. How many heavens will I have invented by the time Ben is grown? That Slow Living guy was right. We need to slow down. We need to avoid being so busy and full of work that we don't have time for ourselves and the delight of thinking about nothing.

I have not thought about nothing in a very long time. I have no idea how to go about it and the thought of it exhausts me—another thing to put on my to-do list that will never come off—

but then it strikes me that Ben thinks about nothing quite a bit and he is pokey as well. There is a role model for the Art of Living Slowly right under my nose! And so begins my secret study of nine-year-olds. After weeks of careful observation of fourth graders in their various habitats: soccer games, birthday parties, the bathroom, car pool and playdates, I have come up with my own list of what I call **The Ninemandments.** These are guaranteed to slow you down and bring you much delight if you choose to live by them.

THE NINEMANDMENTS

1. *Thou shalt begin every sentence with the phrase "No offense, but . . ."*
When you're nine it's okay to insult people to their face. As long as you preface the insult with "No offense, but," no offense can be taken. As in, "No offense, but you suck at four square." Example: You are waiting in line at the pharmacy. The gentleman in front of you does not decline to talk to the pharmacist, as all polite people should when there is a very long line; instead he opts to talk to the pharmacist extensively about his low blood sugar. Is it contagious? Can he pass it on to his wife? Is it safe to have sexual relations with his wife while experiencing low blood sugar? You say, "Excuse me, no offense, sir, but you suck at picking up your medication at Rite-Aid. This is a pharmacy, not a doctor's office." Some situations require two applications of the "no offense" offense, such as: "No offense, buddy, but you're not at death's door. You've got low blood sugar. Eat a Butterfinger."

2. *Thou shalt take twenty minutes to exit the car.*
After the key is pulled out of the ignition just sit there and stare into space vacantly as if you have no idea the car has stopped.

Sway a little bit as if you are still on the highway. Hum, and then burst into song. Sing "Who Stole the Cookie from the Cookie Jar?" Follow this up with Dazz Band's "Let It Whip." Open the door a crack. Wedge your foot out. Then yank your foot back in the car and shut the door completely because you have neglected to take off your seat belt. Take off your seat belt. Eat an old piece of popcorn you find on the floor. Chew it fifty-eight times. Remark to yourself that it tasted like pineapple smoothie. Exit the car. Wonder where everybody went.

3. *Thou shalt be a winner ALL, ALL, ALL the time.*

Because you live in an era and a part of the country where it has been decided that it is very bad to suffer any disappointments or failures of any kind, you shall receive nothing but good news, medals and trophies for everything you do, including contributing to your 401(k) and coughing up the $129 for that Sonic toothbrush. Your medals will be engraved with sayings like: "Chin up! You Came in 10th—That's One Better Than 11th!" and "You'll Always Be a Winner in My Book Even If You Are Really, Really Lazy."

4. *Thou shalt brush thy teeth intermittently (every two to three days).*

Your husband asks you, "Have you brushed your teeth recently?" You say indignantly, "Yes, of course I brushed my teeth." Your husband says, "Did you do a nice job and did you remember to floss?" You say, "Stop asking me if I did a nice job and if I remembered to floss." He says, "Let me see," and you say, "Ahh." He shakes his head, gravely disappointed, and says, "I suggest you go do it again."

5. *Thou shalt write reports filled with haiku, the word* awesome *and the phrase* "You may be interested to know."

EXAMPLE: It is summer and you are full of wonderment. Your

heart and your legs is sore. You need a vacation Band-Aid. But where should you go? May I suggest the great state of Maine, where the state flower is the pinecone tassel and the motto is Eat Lobster Lots of It and Try Not to Think How Much Lobster Looks Like Bugs. You may be interested to know the awesome Stephen King, the famous awesome authoress lives in Maine. His really interesting book *The Shining* scared the crap out of many people and inspired wriders in the world. And now I will finish with a haiku.

Peace, Peace, Peace, Peace, Peace
Peace, Peace, Peace, Peace, Peace, Peace, PEACE
Peace, Peace, Peace, Peace, Peace!!

There are only five Ninemandments. They are called Ninemandments because I learned them from nine-year-olds, not because there are nine of them.

When we moved to Oakland our Realtor told us most houses in the hills didn't have air-conditioning or screens or foundations or crown moldings because nobody was ever home because everybody was always out! Out living their rich, full, active California lives. Imagine! The three of us pale, doughy, light-deprived Maine transplants basking in the insect-free California sun, swimming in outdoor pools all year long.

What our Realtor neglected to tell us was about the rain. It's not widely advertised that in the Bay Area it begins raining in November and doesn't stop until April. February is a volatile mixed bag: trees are flowering and the grass is green, but it can rain for weeks at a time. It's during one of those weeks of nonstop rain that I decide to give this Slow Living a try. What better time to pause than when the winds are at seventy miles per hour and your house is literally shaking on the stilts that tether it to the eroded hillside?

I'm on my elliptical machine when the electricity goes out. I freeze for a moment, waiting for it to flicker back on and when it doesn't I take a long, hot shower. In the past I've found this tactic works well. Use up all the hot water and act like the lights haven't gone out and the lights are fooled into going back on.

The lights don't go back on, and I have to fend off my growing sense of panic. No offense to me, but I suck when the electricity goes off. For some people (my husband and son for instance) it's a great adventure. I feel slightly hysterical, like I am the only one alive in the world and if I could even get to the grocery store (which I can't because every tree in Oakland has fallen down and blocked the road) it would be fruitless, for all that would be left would be toilet brushes and air freshener. I press my face to the window, searching for a bit of blue sky. My husband and son wander past me wearing headlamps.

"I'll have to do my homework by candlelight," says Ben. "You did your homework by candlelight, right, Mom?"

"It's Saturday. You don't have any homework."

"But the lights could be out all weekend. They could be out on Monday, too."

"Well, if that happens you are welcome to do your homework by sconce."

"What's a sconce?"

"A candleholder that hangs on the wall. It's much safer than a candle. Unattended candles are the leading cause of house fires."

Now that we have a fire escape plan I know everything there is to know about fires.

Ben looks at me miserably. The poor kid has no idea what a sconce is. When I was a kid we did our homework by sconce—at least once in a while, as a treat. We used india ink and a quill pen, too. Well, Rebecca did. According to my mother, Dawn and I did not believe in homework. If the electricity went off in 1971 it was no big deal. My mother would just bake cornbread in our beehive oven for supper. She had a really long bread paddle that she sometimes used to spank us with when she wasn't using it to bake corn bread.

"You're lucky spanking went out of style," I tell Ben.

"Can we not talk about that?" he says. "You always bring it up when the lights go out."

It's strange the things you talk about when the lights go out. Things you would never talk about when there is electricity. I've come to realize the electricity going out is the equivalent of drinking half a bottle of Maker's Mark in one second.

"I think we should take it slow today," I say.

"Let's play Monopoly," says Ben.

"Let's light a fire," says my husband.

"Let's go to the mall," I suggest. The mall *always* has electricity.

We have a fabulous time at the mall even though it's unbelievably crowded. People are pleasant and smiling. There's this we're-all-in-this-together kind of feeling that casts everything in a champagne glow. We have dinner at PF Chang's, and for once it doesn't bother me that I have to wait forty-five minutes for a table because we pass that time playing word games and eavesdropping on other people's conversations. If I close my eyes we could be in Umbria, not the Emery Bay Mall. I smile and nod at the people around me like we're all related and have lived in a small medieval village for centuries.

After dinner I while away half an hour choosing between the Oscar Biondi and Bumble and Bumble hair powder at Sephora.

"It's dry shampoo. Just in case the electricity is off for more than a day," I explain to my husband. "Isn't this great? Having no destination? How about we go try and find some gelato?"

"How about we go home," he says.

When we get in the car my husband turns on the radio and I turn it off.

People who are living the Slow Life do not listen to the radio. A hand-cranked radio, maybe.

"Let's sing," I say. " 'Chicks and ducks and geese better scurry.' "

"That sounds like a baby song," says Ben.

"It's not a baby song. Shirley Jones sang it in *Oklahoma*."

I continue, " 'When I take you out in the surrey—' "

"He doesn't know what a surrey is," says my husband.

"It's a kind of carriage," I say.

I sing "The Surrey with the Fringe on Top" by myself until we get to our exit. My husband is busy trying to steer clear of fallen tree branches. The houses in the village are twinkling with lights. I feel lucky to be alive.

"I think we need to live in a different way," I say. "We've forgotten the important things. Maybe we should start celebrating Shabbat. You know, no driving, no watching TV, no working on Saturdays."

"We're not Jewish," says my husband.

"That doesn't mean we couldn't adopt some of their traditions," I say. "I don't think they'd mind. I'll ask Robin."

As soon as we start driving up the hill to our house the wind kicks in and I get a very bad feeling. We live a thousand feet up in a completely different microclimate than five minutes down the hill. Five minutes down the hill all the happy people are watching *CSI* and recharging their toothbrushes. Our neighborhood is eerily dark. Deer and wild turkey trot arrogantly down the middle of the road. How quickly the animals take over.

"I can't believe it," I say. "Still no electricity."

"I think you're going to get your Shabbat," says my husband.

We have rarely been without electricity for more than three hours and we have no idea what to do with ourselves. We would go to bed but it's only seven. My husband lights a fire and we huddle around the laptop watching an inappropriate R movie because it's the only movie we have. We instruct Ben to cover his eyes at the sexy and violent parts (just for good measure I put a pillow over his face) and recite the alphabet loudly so he can't hear the actors making love or killing one another with machetes. Twenty minutes later we shut it off.

"Now what?" I say.

"I miss Bodhi," says Ben.

"I miss him, too," says my husband, putting his arm around Ben.

"I have an idea," I say.

"We are not in the mood to sing," says my husband.

"How about we go for a walk?"

"No, thank you," says Ben, snuggling into his father's armpit.

"There are fifty-mile-an-hour gusts," says my husband.

"Well, I'm going for a walk. It's better than sitting in this cold, dark house."

"Take a rope," says my husband. "Tie yourself to the mailbox and you can rappel down the street."

"Ha-ha," I say.

"At least wear a headlamp," he says.

I can barely walk up the street, but I enjoy the challenge. The force of the wind makes me feel petite—a little slip of a thing that could just be blown away.

My pocket rings. I fish out my cell phone.

"We heard about the storm," says Dawn.

California weather always makes it to the national news. Everyone is happy to know Californians are suffering and clinging to life (or hillsides) just like everybody else in the rest of the country.

"We've been without electricity for nine hours!" I say.

"Nine hours, wow."

"What are you doing up?" I ask her.

"I missed my sleep window."

"What's your sleep window?"

"Eight to eight thirty."

"You fall asleep at eight in the evening?"

"No, I don't fall asleep at eight; I have three boys. What I'm saying is I'd like to fall asleep at eight. Ten years from now when they're all gone I can fall asleep at eight."

"Don't," I say. "Even when you can, don't."

She sighs. "I'm so tired."

"I know you are," I say. "You should go to bed."

"Okay," she yawns.

"Wait, what's it doing there?" I ask her.

I always need weather reports from back home.

"It smells like pine trees and sap and snow and car exhaust. The sky is that deep purple that you only get in winter. I'd tell you the constellations, but I've forgotten the names of all of them except for the Big Dipper. Has that happened to you? Have you forgotten everything?"

"Sort of."

"Are you worried you have Alzheimer's?"

"Yes!" I whisper.

She sighs. "I read somewhere that thirty-five percent of people in their eighties have it, and if you make it to fifty, chances are you'll make it into your eighties," she says. "Either we die in the next seven years or odds are we'll slowly go mad. Now do you blame me for wanting to go to bed at eight?"

I see her point.

"I'm very glad your house hasn't fallen down the cliff and into the bay yet," she says and hangs up.

I go home. I crawl into bed and snuggle up next to my husband. It's freezing. Surely the electricity will be on in the morning.

Good thing you bought that powder hair shampoo," says my husband the next morning.

It's pouring outside. The house is still dark. He's wearing his headlamp again. It appears to be soldered onto his head.

"I can't believe this," I say. "Where the hell is Pacific Gas & Electric?" I count on my fingers. "It's been twenty-one hours without electricity!"

"Think I'll call my mom," he says cheerily.

My mother-in-law lives in rural mid-coast Maine in a little town called St. George.

"Hi, Mom. Yeah, we're having a storm. We've been without electricity for a while."

"Tell her twenty-one hours," I whisper.

"Yeah. Yes. Really? You've been without electricity for five days? Your pipes burst? The toilets are overflowing? When you were outside on your deck you slipped on the ice and broke your collarbone?"

"Give me the phone," I say.

He hands it over. I hear a dial tone.

"Sweetheart, the electricity is out. It's not the end of the world," he says gently.

It may not be the end of the world, but it's the end of something.

When I told my parents we were moving to California they were thrilled for us. What a lark! What an adventure! They would miss us terribly but they would visit. But then, like the snubbed fairy in *Sleeping Beauty,* they set their terms. They didn't tell us that when our son became a teenager he would prick himself on a spindle and die, but close. They said, Go west. Eat the best General Tso's chicken of your life. Sleep without air-conditioning in the dog days of August and enjoy twelve different varieties of tangerines all year round, but you must come back to New England before your son is eight.

Eight—it seemed like such an arbitrary number, but my father quickly rattled off the reasons that would make his grandson particularly vulnerable in his eighth year. Who knew so many potential life-altering conditions had their genesis at eight—things like slouching and buckteeth? But the real reason that could not be spoken of because New Englanders do not speak of such things was that if we stayed any longer it would be too late: we would never return.

My father was right. It is too late for us—we are never going to move back home. Ben is nine and the truth is California has cast its spell on us. We're been seduced by the climate and the rolling hills that look like God's knuckles, the jasmine that blooms on every corner and the man on the street who reminds us to slow down. We may be silly people who live in a house built on stilts. We may be stupid people who live in a house built virtually on top of a fault line, but I ask you, whose house *isn't*? And whose rooms haven't gone dark for days? Which one of us hasn't been shaken so hard by life's temblors that all we can do is fall to our knees, sing songs from *Oklahoma* and count the seconds until it's over? If it hasn't happened to you yet, I'm glad, but I'm sorry to tell you, it will. The good news is the beginning is buried in the rubble of the end.

So you say good-bye best dog there will never be another one like you. Good-bye husband who used to be a mystery. Good-bye toddler who woke up singing every morning and sang himself to sleep every night.

You say hello clean house that is no longer covered in dog hair. Hello husband who will still surprise you if only you let yourself be open to surprises. Hello brokenhearted boy.

Welcome to this world.

March

PEE WEE LACROSSE IS AN ENTIRELY DIFFERENT SPORT THAN SOCCER. YOU don't just throw on a pair of knee socks and shin guards and you're good to go. Instead you must put on a cup (to protect your Wee Pee), chest and elbow pads, gloves, a mouth guard and a helmet and THEN you're ready to throw down. Or get encephalitis from being thrown down. What I am trying to say is *What in the hell was my husband thinking, insisting that I become the mother of a child who plays lacrosse?* Doesn't he know after eighteen years together how completely unfit I am for this job?

I think he has mistaken me for my friend Renee, or Coach Renee, as she is better known around here. It would be easy to see why. Renee and I have a lot in common. Our sons are best friends and are on the same lacrosse team. She is half-Lebanese, I am half-Armenian; we both grew up eating pita bread.

But that's where the similarities end. Renee is a survivor. She became terribly ill right after her son, Parker, was born. She died twice and was brought back to life twice—but she doesn't talk about this much. Most people don't know that she lives with chronic pain because she endures it with a stoicism and grace that is bewildering to me. She has been coaching Parker's soccer team for five years. Her players adore her. Parents seek her out for her levelheaded advice, which is usually along the lines of *Your kid's doing great and will continue to do great if you stop screwing with his head.* I am glad she is my friend because I can count on her to set me straight.

"I don't want to go to the boys' lacrosse game on Saturday," I tell her. "It's too painful."

"Did Ben get hit last game?" she asks.

"No, but he will," I say.

Renee sighs. "You can't sit around worrying if this is the day when he gets hit."

"That's the point. I can't bear the agony of waiting. That's why I don't want to go," I say.

"Well, don't go, then," she says.

"Really?" I say.

"No, not really! Don't you want to be there when he wins?"

"Yes, of course I want to be there when he wins. I just don't want to be there when he loses."

Renee doesn't respond. A good coach knows when to be silent and exactly how much silence is needed to have the stupid thing that has just flown out of your mouth find a way back in.

"It hurts too much," I say.

"It hurts Ben?"

"No, it hurts me! Don't you hate losing?" I ask her.

"They actually learn more from losing than they do from winning," she says.

"But it sucks to lose," I say.

"It sucks more not to be in the game," she says.

The problem is the caste system and that it is so much more delineated in lacrosse than it is in soccer. In lacrosse everyone knows who the A team is even if they don't say it. Lacrosse is a game of statistics. Everything is always being counted—goals and assists and concussions—so the boys know exactly what their ranking is. This is not like recreation league soccer where everybody gets a trophy even if you come in last. Lacrosse is a microcosm of the real world. Out on the field there are rock stars, and there are project managers and garbage collectors and video store clerks, and each boy knows exactly what job he has although some are more vocal about it than others. For instance, the garbage collectors and video clerks tend to keep their career choices to themselves. The rock stars frequently do little shimmies of joy.

Ben adores the game, but he has yet to break out and score a goal. I know he wants one, but in order to get one he'll have to move past my fear.

"He's got my athleticism and your reserve," says my husband.

Which is a nice way of saying Ben got all his gifts from his father and all his neuroses from me.

"Just what do you mean by 'reserve'?" I ask.

"Well, you're not exactly a risk-taker," he says.

"I tore my ACL skiing," I remind him, lifting up my skirt to show him the three-inch scar.

This usually scores me lots of points. People are shocked at the size of the scar and they assume I am a double-black-diamond skier and I do not disabuse them of this notion.

"I was teaching you to ski, we were on the bunny slope, you were doing a pizza wedge and the instant you gained the tiniest bit of speed you screamed and fell on top of me. That's how you tore your ACL," he says.

"It was a serious injury. They had to carry me down in a sled!"

My husband rolls his eyes.

"*Pop!* That's the sound it made. *Twang. Twang.* Like a rubber band."

I read somewhere that's what an ACL tear sounded like, and I had repeated the story often enough that it felt true.

My husband shakes his head. "If you're going to keep this attitude up I don't think you should come to the lacrosse games. You're psyching Ben out."

"How can you say that? I'm a good mother."

"Yes, you are. At everything but sports," he says. "You're horrible at sports."

"That's not nice," I say.

"Well, it's true," he says.

"But it's so in-your-face," I say. "Everybody wanting to WIN, WIN, WIN! Is this what it's like to be a boy?"

"This is what it's like to be alive," he says.

There are lots of things I used to do that I don't do anymore: climb trees, dive, ski, ride my bicycle. These activities used to bring me a lot of joy. Now I can barely imagine doing them.

The diving and tree climbing I don't miss so much because, honestly, how many opportunities does a forty-four-year-old woman have to dive and climb trees? And because I wrecked my knee I figure I have a free pass to never ski again. But the biking haunts me because we live in paradise. People come from all around the Bay Area to bike in my neighborhood. It's very hard to see the bikers and not feel inadequate, so instead I make fun of them: those ridiculous hornet-men helmets, that skintight clothing. Have you ever met a more entitled group? Hogging the road. Zipping through red lights. Waving their fists at you angrily when all you were trying to do was get past them on that blind curve.

The last time I was on a bike was in Maine in 1989. My husband and I had just met, and he took me home to meet his parents. He thought it would be nice to ride to Port Clyde and get a lobster roll at the Dip Net. It was a lovely outing for my husband, as he was riding his father's twenty-speed bike. It was much less lovely for me, as I was riding his mother's no-speed bike in a pair of clogs. What my husband had neglected to tell me was that Port Clyde was a peninsula away. I recall sobbing uncontrollably on the side of the highway. I may even have made him pedal me ten miles home on his handlebars.

This kind of behavior was okay when I was single. But now that I am a mother it's not. Just yesterday Ben said to me, "It really isn't cool if you fall down and cry and then you say the F word."

He claimed he was talking about a classmate, but I'm pretty sure he was talking about me when I fell on my butt on the stairs, so hard the tears welled up in my eyes, and I said *fuck fuck fuck fuck fuck* five times because it felt good to have a reason to say *fuck* so many times in a row.

I asked Ben what should you do when you fall down.

He said, "Get the F up."

I was thinking more along the lines of weep. I was also thinking of the future, when some kid in lacrosse checked him so hard he flew into the goalpost and cracked his skull open, so I said, "What if you're really hurt? What if you get hit so hard your arm breaks?"

He said, "Why are you such a pessimist? Why do you always think the sky is falling?"

"Have you been eavesdropping on your father and me?"

Ben shrugged. "Maybe the sky is calling, not falling."

I have never been on the A team, but I know all about being on the B team due to the fact I have been on it since I was in the womb. Born two minutes after Dawn (who I am convinced bit me and then shoved me aside in her haste to get out before me), I found that my first official name was Twin B.

Dawn was the jock. We competed in everything: gymnastics, being allergic to poison ivy and growing boobs, and she beat me at all these things. The one thing I was faster than her at was reading. I was the girl who wandered through the woods with her notebook, spying on people, the girl who slurped down bowls of rice pudding and in her free time blackmailed Suzy Tucker into giving up her homemade sugar cookies.

When I was in fifth grade I had my breakthrough. I wrote an essay about a father giving his three-year-old daughter a bath. I was inspired by an ad for towels I found in my parents' *Town & Country* magazine and my longing for a simpler time when I did not have so much homework. I wrote about the softness of the towel and the sun pouring in through the window and the girl's dimpled knees and the love the father felt for his daughter.

When my teacher, Ms. Mania (I kid you not, and she lived up to her name—she often ran out of the classroom in tears) read it, she told me I had a gift. Finally I had something none of my sisters had: a knack for stringing words together. I would have preferred a knack for the balance beam or telepathy, but at least I had a knack for something.

If I had known what my knack had in store for me—a lifetime membership to the B team—I would have denied authorship of that essay. I would have said it was Dawn's. She was the writer. She was the one who longed to be three again because life was so easy when you didn't have hair on your legs and unrequited crushes on boys named Billy and Jimmy, when the worst thing that could happen to you was to find a spider in your bed.

But it was too late. I had gotten my first taste of celebrity: the "A" scrawled in violet pen on my paper, Ms. Mania reading my work out loud to the class. It was my first invitation to the dance. Sure, I would go to the dance and be ignored, but at least I got invited.

A few years ago I made the mistake of thinking I had moved up. I had recently published a book for young adults and as a result of good reviews and some local press I was invited to be on an authors' panel at Book Group Expo. I didn't say it to anyone, but I was thinking my time had finally come. After all these years I had finally made it to the A team.

My friend Joanne accompanied me. We pretended she was my media escort so she could get in for free. I received a special name tag that said AUTHOR, a bag full of literary swag, and a backstage pass to the Authors' Green Room.

The Authors' Green Room! Who could have imagined such a thing? I parted ways with Joanne, stepped over the threshold and was immediately transported back to grade school. Everybody seemed to know everybody. They were huddled in groups, whispering and laughing. Panicked, I went straight for the refreshment table. As I was looking at the array of bottled waters, a flashbulb went off in my eyes. Paparazzi!

Whenever I am being photographed I become incredibly self-conscious and I figure the best thing to do so I don't appear vain is to pretend I have no idea I am being photographed. There were more flashes. I stood still, a serious look on my face, thinking deep Author thoughts like *Holy shit, somebody is taking my picture!* There was another voice in my head, a voice that I ignored that said, *Melanie, honestly, why would anybody be taking* your *picture?* More clicks of the shutter. I turned my head to the left and subtly tossed my hair.

"Thank you, ZZ," said a voice.

"No problem," said the woman next to me.

I was standing next to ZZ Packer, who clearly had no problem smiling for the camera as she had so much experience being photographed. She smiled at me and said hello. I shuffled away, riddled with shame and envy.

I should have left right then. I should have found Joanne and made her take me out to lunch, she being my media escort and all. Instead I took a closer look at my schedule and saw much to my horror that at the same time as my panel discussed "The Lure of the Young Adult Novel" in Salon B, fiction royalty Andrew Sean Greer, ZZ and Sara Gruen (whose book *Water for Elephants* had just catapulted her through the literary stratosphere) would be talking about "Where Do You Get Your Ideas" in Salon A.

I tried some coping thoughts.

Nobody is going to make fun of you.
I'll just pretend I'm not afraid.
I have friends, too.

And look, there's a friend right there! Joanne arrived early to the panel and sat in the front row. She gave me a thumbs-up and started looking through the schedule. I was buoyed by the fact that Salon B was a vast room, filled with hundreds of chairs. That was a good sign, right? It meant they were expecting a big crowd. I was nervous, but I was prepared. I knew exactly what I wanted to talk about: why I'd chosen to write for kids, despite kiddie lit's second-class reputation in the literary world, despite the pathetic advances, despite the pitying look I got when I told people I was a writer and they asked what kind of a writer and I told them a children's book author and they asked if I wrote with a crayon.

I planned on telling the audience that I wrote for kids because the books I read when I was a child saved my life. They showed me I could grow a second skin if my own skin was too thin or the wrong color. They made me into what I couldn't be in my real life: brave, bold, and preternaturally fast. I wanted to give this back. I wanted those children who felt exiled, whose talents were yet to be appreciated, whose gifts had yet to surface to know that one day it would be their turn.

People slowly started filtering into the room.

Joanne came up to the dais.

"Did you see who's in Salon A?" she asked.

"I know. Can you believe it?" I whispered.

"Do you mind if I go?"

"Go where?"

"To Salon A," she said.

I tried to keep the same blank look on my face I'd had when I thought I was being photographed by the paparazzi, but I'm not sure how successful I was at keeping my jealousy at bay. Andrew Sean Greer's *The Confessions of Max Tivoli* was one of the few books I had ever read as an adult that had transported me so entirely that as soon as I finished it I read it again. I adored him.

"Of course not. You've heard this all before. I'd be there, too, if I wasn't on this panel," I said.

"I'll take notes. I'll write everything down," she promised. "And I'll meet up with you for the book signing."

While I watched her bolt out of the room, I thought of poor Ms. Mania. What was going on with her that spring of 1973? What must it have been like for her, having to endure listening to *Free to Be . . . You and Me* hundreds of times? And how old was she anyway? She seemed ancient to my eleven-year-old eyes. But she could have been in her twenties for all I knew. Perhaps she had a beautiful voice. Perhaps her dream was to be a singer, the next Joni Mitchell, and instead she was stuck teaching smelly fifth graders.

I wish I could tell you what we discussed: that it was a lively conversation, that I was triumphant in inspiring my audience, that an audience that filled more than the first four rows of chairs was there to hear it. Instead I was in my own private hell, listening through the skimpy walls to the hundreds of people in Salon A roaring with laughter and clapping wildly. I cursed myself for being such a fool. Could my B team status be any clearer? Sure, the B was tarted up with *Salon,* but it was B all the same. Halfway through the panel a group of women wandered into our room, and my heart lifted. Here finally was the crowd: a little late, maybe there was a long line in the ladies' room? But very quickly these women realized they had mistaken Salon B for Salon A and high-tailed it out of there.

Should I tell you about the further humiliation of the book signing, where all the authors sit in one room behind desks with piles of their books in front of them, pens in hand? Should I tell you about my nonexistent line and the painfully long lines for ZZ, Sara and Andrew who were laughing it up with their fans? Fans that my loyal media escort, Joanne, was doing her best to steal away and send over to me.

"She wrote an amazing children's book. It's about a boy whose face is burned off in a fire," she told them.

"We're here for Luis Alberto Urrea," they said.

"It sounds a little dark," they said.

"Is it illustrated?" they asked.

"Sure, there's illustrations. A really neat one of a boy going up in flames," I heard Joanne lie to some woman.

"You can stop now," I said to Joanne. "Your escorting services are no longer needed."

"I'm sorry," she said. "Do you want me to tell you this amazing thing that Andy said?"

"Andy who?"

"Andrew Sean Greer."

"People call him Andy?"

"Well, his friends do," said Joanne.

I didn't need Joanne to tell me what Andy said because I could imagine it. He probably said something along the lines of how he couldn't believe this was happening to him. How it all felt so surreal and out of his control and all he could do was go along for the ride. How all his life he had sat on the bench and now this quirky, eloquent, breathtaking book about a man who ages in reverse had brought him here, where he sat on a stage speaking to hundreds of people whose faces were lit up like astronauts who had just seen the earth from outer space for the first time.

I am allowed to go to the lacrosse game as long as I promise not to fill Ben's mind with doubt or encourage him to quit—two things I am already guilty of. I find this is easiest to accomplish if I sit by myself far up in the bleachers because the closer I am to the field and to the other parents, the higher my anxiety and the higher the likelihood that I will misbehave.

I am extremely competitive. I want our team to win so badly that I feel sick. Surely there must be other parents who feel the same way. I look at them down below me, waiting for the game to begin. My husband and Renee are eating bagels and sitting at the scorekeeper's table. One father is listening to his transistor radio. A mother is knitting. Do they think this is a picnic?

The game starts and the other team scores a goal immediately, then another goal, and then another. I have a very bad feeling. If I can tear myself away from that bad feeling for a moment, I can see that lacrosse is a beautiful game. The way the boys pass and throw and hurl the ball at the net. The way they call out each other's names and bump chests when they score. I only wish it was our team that was bumping chests. I only wish it was my son who was scoring.

It's clear to me within five minutes that our team is about to be crushed. Each time the other team scores, their parents stand up and cheer. After about the eighth goal I cover my ears. They know their team is going to win. Shouldn't they show some compassion to us poor parents whose kids are such losers? Don't they know that sometimes it is more relaxing for both parents and players to keep your mouth shut?

I take out my notebook. I do this sometimes when I need distance from a situation. I pretend I'm a reporter covering the event. It helps me to stay objective.

Lacrosse Mom Loses It Big in the Bleachers

Next Time Stay Home, beg husband and son

OAKLAND, CALIFORNIA—"That woman was asking for it," reported Melanie Gideon last Saturday. "I mean, how many times did she expect me to hear her yelling, 'Nice job, Ulysses! Way to juke him out. Way to score, you little scoremeister!' before I lost it?"

"It was only a little slap," she added. "Perhaps if she'd been wearing her mouth guard that tooth wouldn't have got busted."

Gideon, who was strong-armed into being a Lacrosse Mom by her husband and her friend Renee, who said what a great experience it would be for their sons to wear a cup and, best of all, have an excuse to whack other boys with sticks, said, "Even though I hit her, I'm not sorry. Being a Lacrosse Mom is not for wimps. You have to expect you're going to get hit. It's that kind of a game."

According to her husband, Gideon was always a wuss—rarely willing to step outside her comfort zone.

"I thought it would be really good for her to see our son get battered around. Maybe break an arm or leg," said her husband. "Incur a little brain damage. Reversible, of course."

"I keep telling her she's got to get into the game," said Renee. "She can't sit in the bleachers forever."

"I'm glad I pushed myself," said Gideon.

She took a knee as the sobbing woman she slugged in the face was led off the field by her husband, who was speed-dialing their dentist.

Gideon stood and wiped her bloody hands on her jeans. "It's important to set an example for my son. Being a Lacrosse Mom was the most challenging job I've ever had, but I didn't quit. I pushed through my fear."

Gideon reports that after this success, she's ready to be a Cricket Mother, Rugby Mother and Competitive Ping-Pong Mom. "Ling it," she said.

"Bring it," translated her husband.

He held out his hand. Gideon spit out her mouth guard.

We lose 12–0. We lose by so much it's almost like winning, and the losing quickly metamorphoses into what an honor it is to play such an amazing team. The more evolved parents begin complimenting the winning team in earnest, showing what good sports they are.

"Well, they certainly can pass."

"What a shot!"

"Man, that kid's got wheels."

Nobody seems depressed except me.

"Nice game," says my husband when Ben walks off the field.

I don't believe in lying to children. "You guys sucked," I say to Ben.

No, of course I didn't really say that, but that's what I thought.

*

That afternoon the doorbell rings. It's my friend Kerri. She is from Mexico, Maine, which tells you everything you need to know. She has biked ten miles to get to my house so we can go for a hike.

A while ago my husband got my bike tuned up for me as a surprise. I had been saying that I really should try biking on an actual road, especially since I had taken up spinning class, but I was kidding. The bike had been sitting in the entryway for months.

"Does that thing work?" asks Kerri.

I pinch the tires. "They're flat."

"They're not flat," says Kerri. "Let's go for a ride."

"I don't think so."

"Why not?"

"Because I'm scared. People run bikers off the road all the time."

"What people?"

"People who are annoyed by bikers and their holier-than-thou ways."

"People like you?" asks Kerri. "Get your lazy ass on the bike."

The ride starts off badly, as we have to bike up a hill.

"Just take your time. Get into a rhythm," says Kerri.

I'm panicked. Hills terrify me. You have to work so hard to get up them.

"If it's too steep you can get off the bike and walk," says Kerri.

That has never occurred to me. Isn't that—cheating? "Are you sure?"

"Absolutely," says Kerri.

I hop off the bike and push it up the hill. When we get to the top I get back on and slowly we ride down the road. I inhale deeply. The air smells like mulch and bay leaves.

"Beautiful day," says a man on a bike as he passes us.

"Yes!" we cry.

Suddenly I am seized with happiness. He thinks I'm like him. I am passing as a woman who knows a kind of happiness and freedom that only bikers know. How could I have ever hated them?

Soon I begin to ride two or three days a week. I quickly learn that the reason bicyclists ride in the middle of the street is most times they can't hear cars coming up behind them, what with the wind whistling in their ears and those helmets.

I start giving bikers a wide berth when I'm in my car. I tap on my horn lightly to let them know I'm behind them. I wave at them in solidarity.

"Nice day for a ride," I yell at them, but what I'm really yelling is *I'm one of you.*

I have a bit of Post-Traumatic Hills Syndrome from when my husband forced me to do that ten-mile ride, so every time I approach a hill and feel that familiar pressure building in my chest, the panic at the thought of all the hard work I'm about to be forced to do, I just remind myself to put it in the lowest gear and pedal, and when I do this I notice things. The way the sun beats through the vents on my helmet. The way fellow cyclists zip past me and shout hello and don't judge me for going too slow or having the wrong kind of bike. Sometimes I pedal and look up, just for a moment, and think of what Ben said—that the sky is calling, not falling. I dare to think the day may come when I like hills more than coasting, but that might be pushing it.

Are you sure you don't want to come to the game?" asks my husband a week later.

"I've got to do the bills," I say. "Besides it's so early."

Who schedules lacrosse games at eight on Saturday mornings? The truth is I can't bear to see them lose again, so my plan is to just stay home—for the rest of the season.

An hour later my husband texts me. "Ben just got a goal!"

Can I tell you how ridiculously happy I am for him? For me? For all of us? How I leap out of the chair and do a little shimmy of joy. I pump my fist in the air, something I've watched other parents do when their kids get goals. I can't believe this means so much, but it does.

And then a few minutes later my husband texts me again. "He just got another one!"

This time I cry. I missed seeing my son scoring his first lacrosse goals ever. I missed seeing him throw his hands up in the air in triumph and bump chests with his teammates.

I think about what Renee asked me: "Don't you want to be there when he wins?"

The only way I will be there to see him win is if I am willing to be there when he loses. Every single time he loses. My job is to not look away.

A few days later Renee's husband, Mike, calls and tells me Renee is not having a good day and she can't come on the family bike ride we had planned. What this means is that the pain is so bad she's bedridden. It's a beautiful day—she urges us to go without her.

The five of us—my husband, Ben, Mike, his son, Parker, and

I—set out on the Moraga bike trail. The first half of the ride is downhill and the path winds through fields and meadows. But what goes down must go up. The boys don't want to ride all the way back, so we leave my husband with the kids and Mike and I bike back up to the parking lot to get the car.

If I had a brother I would want him to be just like Mike. He's one of the sweetest men I know—kind and generous with a mean swearing streak. We are talking about food. It's a kind of last hurrah, because on Monday we are both starting diets. We've already talked extensively about donuts and cream puffs and morning buns. Now we've moved on to cookies.

"Have you ever tried freezing Fudge Stripe Cookies?" he asks.

"Jesus, that's brilliant," I say.

"They get crispy. They just break into pieces," he says. "Like peanut brittle."

And then our handlebars get tangled up.

Kids are no strangers to the scraped knee and the bee bite, poison ivy pustules and broken fingers. But when you're an adult, falling is unexpected. You think you're too old to fall. Until you do.

Mike detaches his bike from mine and veers off to the left. But I can't recover and I fall. An old lady fall, not an athletic fall, by which I mean I let out a kind of eagle caw, *AHHHHH,* and am suspended in midair for what seems like a minute, during which time I am thinking, *I am falling, how did this happen, I can't believe I'm falling, this is going to hurt, fuck, this is going to hurt* and then I'm sprawled on the ground.

The first thing everybody asks me when I show them the impressive scrape on my elbow and my calf (which over the next week will swell into a stump, black and blue and purple and red and yellow), is *Did you cry?* No, I didn't cry. I screamed in anticipation of what was coming, but I didn't cry. Sure, my elbow was streaming blood and stung like hell and my leg was numb, but I felt grateful because I was here. In this day. Inside of this moment. The bike path was dappled with sun. People stopped to help me. Soon it would be dusk and I would have a nice glass of wine. I got back on the bike and pedaled uphill for the next five miles.

You should have heard her," says Mike to my husband once we circled back in the car to pick them up. "She sounded like a deer screaming."

"You don't need to tell me. I've heard that scream before," says my husband, who is about to pour hydrogen peroxide on my elbow and then pick the gravel out with a pair of tweezers.

"Will this hurt?" I ask him.

I think of Renee in her bed on this beautiful Saturday afternoon—just happy to be on the team—any team, A or B. Just so long as she's out on the field.

"Close your eyes," he says.

I shake my head. The days of closing my eyes are over.

April

EVERY TIME I PULL INTO THE CAR POOL LINE TO PICK BEN UP FROM SCHOOL I have this strange sensation that I've just left the car pool line. My entire life is structured around 3:20 p.m. Unfortunately it's the same for millions of other mothers. If you are not a mother with young children (children you cannot force to walk two miles home because things like that are now against the law), I suggest you avoid the roads from 2:45 to 3:30 unless it is absolutely necessary. If you find yourself on the road at this time do not blame me for the weaving Subaru Outback flying past you at top speed driven by the manic woman who is wondering what the hell ever happened to buses?

I can act inappropriately on the freeway, where I have anonymity. But once I approach the exit to school I have to behave. I can't cut people off. Nor can I tailgate, because from the back they might look like strangers but from the front they turn out to be Ben's sensei, so instead I let that woman in the Prius who is actually carpooling (by this I mean bringing home children that aren't her own) into the stream of traffic. I wave, but inside I'm thinking, Hurry the fuck up. I'm in such a hurry to wait in the stifling hot car for thirty minutes because that's how early I have to arrive to be first in car pool line, which is a very nice place to be because honestly, how many opportunities does one have to be first in anything?

Did I mention my son's school is next door to a Mormon temple? It's a very lovely and serene place. There are fountains and elaborate gardens, spires and bridges. When Ben was in kindergarten he asked me when I was going to take him to the amusement park down the street from his school. When I told him it was a church he didn't believe me.

"What kind of a church has rides and castles?" he asked.

"Mormon churches," I told him.

"I'm a Mormon," he said.

"No, you're not," I said.

"Well, what am I?" he asked.

"You're a boy," I said. "A very nice, kind boy."

"I'm a Mormon," he whispered, his eyes filling with tears.

I have a little secret. How I pass the time when sitting in the car pool line. I use a little something my husband gave to me for Valentine's Day. It's called a StressEraser. And no he didn't think of it himself. What kind of a husband would give his wife a StressEraser on Valentine's Day? The kind of husband who wishes never to have sex again? But imagine the conversation if he did.

"I can't wait to open the present you got me for Valentine's Day."

"Wait, don't tell me. Let me guess."

"That topaz necklace I saw at Pavé? You remembered topaz is my birthstone!"

"No? Okay—those fleece pajamas I saw in the Garnet Hill catalog?"

"No? Okay—a box of those amazing sea salt caramels?"

"*I* said I was stressed out? When did I say I was stressed out?"

"You paid *how much* for this?"

The StressEraser is not really an eraser. It's a biofeedback device. It works like so: You stick your finger in it. It reads your pulse. It tells you when to inhale. It tells you when to exhale. That's it. But here's the brilliant part. Within five minutes of doing it you feel like you've drunk half a bottle of wine. And it's legal! And you can do it anywhere. On a park bench. At the doctor's office. In the car pool line. But what the literature doesn't tell you is that it's really, really embarrassing if anybody catches you at it. So I hide the thing under the steering wheel and try to pretend nothing illicit is going on as I slump further and further down in my seat, my stress erased to the point where I'm practically on the ground.

It has occurred to me that I might be mistaken for somebody who is masturbating, because people who masturbate in cars slump, too. Every few minutes I wave my hands around in case anybody is looking and getting the wrong idea. But then I remember some people can orgasm hands-free. Probably most of those people live right here in California.

What am I hiding? What don't I want people to know? That I have stress? That I get anxious? There's a rap on my window. It's my friend Lisa. I've done a hundred breaths. This is supposed to be your entire daily total of breaths and I'm so relaxed I'm not sure I'm capable of speech. I gently toss the StressEraser on the floor.

"Move over," Lisa says, opening the door and sliding in.

Lisa is a therapist. I keep asking her for a name of a therapist and she keeps saying she'll think about it and give me one and she keeps not giving me one and so I keep asking, knowing it's highly unlikely I'll ever get a name. Which is fine with me. I don't really want to go. Certainly not now when I can erase my stress all on my own.

I tuck the StressEraser under the floor mat with my foot. I must protect Lisa. It would be horrible if she found out that a silver box the size of a transistor radio could replace her. Of course if she did I would be sure to remind her that the special patient population would always be in need of a therapist (those with asthma or heart conditions or dead) because proper use of the StressEraser requires breathing.

"Are you high?" she says.

"No, I'm not high," I say, blinking my way out of my stupor.

"What's wrong with you?"

"I've been napping," I tell her.

"I'd nap, too, if I got here an hour early," she says. "So what are you bringing for dinner on Saturday night?"

Lisa and I are part of a small group of women who get together every couple of months or so for dinner. We call ourselves the Flans. Not because we love flan but because our first dinner was in honor of Bastille Day. We spoke schoolgirl French, made crepes and did the Flan-Flan and, well, you get the picture. The name stuck. I for one am glad. Otherwise we would still be calling ourselves *a small group of women who get together every couple of months or so for dinner.*

I sigh. "Is there a theme?"

Many of the Flans are amazing cooks. For weeks now we've been e-mailing back and forth about what everybody is bringing for dinner. We start with a main dish and then people riff off that. I've been mostly silent for two reasons: I'm not sure I'm going to make it and the only thing I can reliably make is salad.

"Just bring salad," says Lisa.

"I will if I can come," I say.

"You're coming," says Lisa.

"No, really, I'm not sure I can."

I explain that I'll be out of town that day and just getting back at dinnertime, assuming everything goes smoothly and there's no traffic.

"You have to come," says Lisa. "You don't have to bring anything. Come late. Just come."

There's a part of me that likes having an out. I enjoy our Flan dinners, but our burgeoning intimacy scares me. I used to think I was a touchy-feely kind of person. It turns out I'm not. Sometimes I think my husband and I have reversed genders. He's much more nurturing. Softer with Ben. He's compassionate and generous; he cooks and loves unconditionally.

I am much more withholding. It's easier for me to love in the abstract. I can take little sips of intimacy, like a good wine, but I hold the wine in my mouth for a long time before I swallow. Then I say *Yikes, that was an amazing wine. I want to drink that wine forever.* By which time the bottle is usually empty.

Kids start to straggle by.

"Gotta go," says Lisa. "So I'll see you Saturday night."

"I'll try," I say.

A few minutes later I see Ben walking up the hill. His posture changes from second to second, almost like he can't quite remember who he is. He flits from running (school is out!) to shoulders slumped (I got picked fourth for soccer) to melodramatic belly clutching (maybe I can convince Mom to buy me a Snickers). When he spies me, he can't help the expression streaming over his face. Relief. Happiness. She came back! I feel it, too. It's ridiculous, I know—he's not an infant. But it's primal. Every day I forget what it costs to separate, but I remember as soon as I see that beloved, hopeful face.

I know these days are numbered. That in the not too distant future there will be no smiling, just scowling, and perhaps some grunts because he will be so weighed down with burdens of homework and social pressures and embarrassment of me. That detachment is coming. Perhaps it's already there, calling sweetly to him after I've tucked him into bed at night.

Ben climbs in the car. "Jesus, I forgot my sweater," he says, meeting my eyes in the rearview mirror.

"Did you just say *Jesus*?" I say.

He claps his hand over his mouth. "Sorry."

"Does your father say *Jesus*? Fuck. You've got to stop saying *Jesus*. It's not appropriate for a nine-year-old to say. Do you ever say that in school? Please tell me you don't say that at school."

"I forgot my sweater."

"Jesus! That's a forty-dollar sweater."

I think it's time for me to go back to therapy. Not only am I stressed out and anxious but I also have insomnia. Every night for the past week I've woken up at two in the morning. I've taken to going outside on our deck and curling up on the chaise lounge with a blanket. Then I lie there and think of all the things I want: the list is endless. And all the things that I thought I wanted but it turned out I didn't, which is most things, like that third helping of pad thai and those green Frye boots. Then I think of all the things I should want, if I were a better person, but I don't, like the banning of plastic bags and quarterly reports of my credit rating.

I've had mixed experiences with therapy. I sought out my first therapist in college. She was a Jungian analyst. I learned a great deal from her in our one appointment. I learned that if my mental health was really important to me I'd find a way to pay her $360-a-month fee on my $500-a-month cocktail waitress income that had to cover rent, food, and any other incidentals as well as exploring the meaning of the recurring dream where my brain drains out of my ear.

I found my second therapist on the bulletin board of a grocery store. *Discover your power animals,* read the ad. *Find your purpose in life through Native American wisdom.* And the most important bit of information: *Sliding scale.* I called right away. The woman's voice sounded just as I'd imagined it would. She was grandmotherly but comforting and firm. I wanted to yell on the phone, What's my animal? Tell me now! It's the bear, right? And if not the bear then the mountain lion, or the eagle? But I controlled myself. I felt she was keeping information from me, information she could divine simply by listening to the timbre of my voice, but I kept my mouth shut. I was afraid she wouldn't take me on.

I could barely wait for my appointment. I stopped dreaming about my brain leaking out of my head. Instead I began dreaming of my therapist. The wise old Native American woman who would be guiding me. Who would send me on vision quests.

Quests with very little food (perhaps I'd lose some weight!) but accompanied by my animal guides. I would learn why I was here. What I was meant to do. Why I was compelled to show up thirty minutes early to every appointment.

And it was a good thing I did. I had the wrong address. It *had* to be the wrong address. This was not the house of a tribal elder. It was a house of babies and toddlers. I could hear them screaming in the backyard. I checked my notes. No, this was it. Perhaps my therapist lived by the old ways. Perhaps she lived in a kind of village, with her daughter and grandchildren! I loved this idea. In theory anyway. It wouldn't work for me. I am an Indian, but the wrong kind of Indian (my father is from Hyderabad) and a Rhode Island Indian to boot, which means, for all intents and purposes, not into communal living of any sort.

The woman who greeted me at the door looked barely older than me. And she was white. The apprentice, I thought. Most shamans I had read about had an apprentice. In fact, I had hoped that after years of working with this woman I would go from client to apprentice. Once I proved my worth. Once I was living my power-animal life. Then I saw her buckskin suede boots. She was holding a bundle of sage. The room behind her was full of dream catchers and medicine shields.

"Have you ever been smudged?" she asked.

"Uh, no," I said.

"Don't be afraid," she said.

She lit the sage and then, when the bundle was smoking, she waved it around my face. At first it was pleasant and it made me think of cowboys and the high country. Then the aroma turned acrid.

"It smells kind of like pot," I said to her.

She just smiled and continued making large sweeping motions with the burning bundle, while explaining to me that working with her would improve my connection to The Great Mystery, that the gifts of true healing medicine are free (except for the $35 fee we negotiated) and now that I was thoroughly smudged it was time to pick my power animals.

She snuffed the sage bundle in a seashell. Out came a deck of cards. She began shuffling.

"Wait—I'm going to pick my totem animals from a deck of cards?" I asked her.

I had expected that through our telephone conversation and now meeting me in person she would know all about me. She would say to herself, *That is a coyote woman if ever I've seen one. Look how the spirit of the coyote fills her. Invisible of course to everybody but me. Now I must tell her. The burden and the gifts of the coyote. The wisest and most powerful of creatures. What strong medicine this young woman has. I think I will ask her to be my apprentice.*

"Of course not," she said, fanning out the deck of cards. "They are going to pick you."

"No, you mean I am going to pick them," I said. "Arbitrarily."

She lit the sage and smudged me again, to get rid of my negative energy, and explained that I had nine totem animals. I should shut my eyes and focus and ask the animals to come to me. Then I should pick a card that I was drawn to.

I did as she said. I shut my eyes and I prayed.

Please don't let me pick the beaver. Oh, please, God, don't let me pick the beaver. Power. Power. Power. Also not the frog. You know I am not a frog person. I have been walking the Good Red Road all my life, so no weasels either. I am your servant, Earth

Mother. Anything but a grouse. Not that I don't like grouses. So great that you made them. I mean, really, how did you think that up?

My hand hovered over a card. I felt energy rising from it and smacking me in the face. She was right! The animal was picking me!

"This one," I whispered.

"Yes," whispered my therapist. *"Yes!"*

I picked it up and turned it over.

It was the turkey.

I continued going to this therapist for many years. Our sessions went a little like this.

"So and so has betrayed me."

"Well, what would opossum do in this instance?"

Screw opossum, I would think. I hate that little rodent. Why did it have to be one of my nine totem animals?

"Opossum would play dead," my therapist would gently suggest.

"I don't understand. What good would that do me? Shouldn't I confront so and so?"

"Or run away."

"I am not the kind of person who runs away."

"You are thinking like a two-legged. Think like a four-legged, or a creepy-crawler, or a finned one, or a winged one," she suggested.

"I think it might be time for me to go on a vision quest," I said, looking around the basement. I could hear her kids through the ceiling. There was a large bump and somebody started to cry.

"I think that's a great idea!"

"Really?"

"Yes, you can go on one right now. Shut your eyes. Let me just go get the cards."

Recently I sought out a cognitive behavioral therapist (CBT). At our initial appointment, I gave her my laundry list of neuroses, and she said she thought we could work through them in two months. Two months! All I had to do was something called Risk Assessments whenever my worrying got out of control.

Here was my first Risk Assessment:

Feared Event: Getting to the car pool line late.
Automatic Thoughts: Fuck those people who are in front of me.
Rate Anxiety from 0 to 100: 95
Predict the Worst Possible Consequences: I'm fiftieth in line. Child is
   dead by the time he finds the car.
Possible Coping Thoughts: Somebody has to be fiftieth in line.
   Why can't I be okay with being fiftieth?
Possible Coping Actions: Get right back in the car pool line after
   dropping child off in the morning.
Re-rate Anxiety from 0 to 100: 94

I went a little overboard with the Risk Assessments. I risk-assessed everything from going to the bathroom in public toilets to getting my eyebrows waxed. CBT made me even more stressed out, as I was constantly checking in with myself, monitoring my mood, thoughts and feelings. It wasn't long before I found myself longing for my medicine cards days, so I sought out the wisdom of Turkey, the patron saint of gobbling. Turkey told me to quit therapy and instead spend that weekly hour eating dried fried crispy shrimp at Shen Hua. It appeared I had picked the right totem animal after all.

It's a few days before our Flan gathering, and e-mails are flying furiously back and forth. The meal is being built like an Amish barn raising, the skeleton of the structure lying flat on the ground, but everybody can see the glorious thing that it will be once it is hauled up—the way it will lean into the sky. Someone is making bagna cauda. Someone else pate en croute. There will be almond soup from the *Moosewood Cookbook*. Éclairs from La Farine and a separate cheese course with exquisite cheeses from the Berkeley Cheese Board. I have decided I'm not going, but I haven't told everybody yet. I have a good excuse. Chances are I won't be back in time, and even if I were I'd be in a bad mood from all that driving and traffic.

I do this kind of waffling a lot. I think to myself, *Wouldn't you really rather stay home?* And most of the time the answer is yes. I long for community, yet I shy away from intimacy. And then I wonder why, despite all the fine people in my life, I am so lonely. The kind of lonely I have no right to feel. Especially since I go to sleep every night next to a man I love. Especially since I have a child whom I adore, whose needs, even at the age of nine, fill my days. But the truth is sometimes I am the kind of lonely that one does not speak about because if you did nobody would want to be near you.

My friend, Laura, who is an acupuncturist, told me that life is devotion, not a pursuit.

"What do you mean, 'devotion'?" I asked her.

"In Chinese medicine the wound is the wanting," she explained. "The wound is desire."

"But how do you stop desiring?" I asked.

"Say *yes*. With every breath," she said. "Make *yes* your prayer."

The next day as I'm driving home from dropping Ben off at school, I spontaneously pull into the parking lot of the Mormon temple. I get that same illicit feeling I do when I'm using the StressEraser—as if I'm hiding something and I'm about to be caught. I get out of the car anyway and walk into the beautifully manicured gardens.

The temple is an awesome sight. It rises majestically into the air, and even though I am a nonbeliever I swear I feel something—a kind of opening, a longing.

The temple has five spires, is made of Sierra White Granite and looks like Cinderella's castle. I can see why Ben thought it was Disneyland. The grounds are also spectacular and offer up a panoramic view of San Francisco and the bay. There are fountains, a little wooden bridge, and a central walkway lined with palm trees. I'm about to leave when a young woman comes toward me and asks, "Do you mind if I walk with you?"

I'd heard from friends that they were hit on the moment they set foot on the temple grounds. But I thought this early in the morning I could walk around unnoticed.

"Okay, but I'm leaving," I say, not wanting to be rude.

"I'll walk you to your car," she says firmly.

Have they been spying on me? Is she an escort? Have I done something wrong?

"Is it okay that I'm here?" I ask.

"Oh, yes," she says. "The grounds are open to the public. You can come back anytime."

"I'll do that," I say, having no intention of ever coming back.

"Do you know where you're going?" she asks.

"My car is right there," I say, pointing.

"No, I mean do you know where you're going?" she repeats.

"After this?" I ask.

"Yes, after this," she says.

"I'm going to Lucky's," I say.

She smiles. "After Lucky's?"

"Home."

"After home?"

"I've got to go."

I drive off like a fugitive, my heart pounding. What was I thinking, going in there? *Did I know where I was going?* Well, yes. Now I am going to Colonial Donuts to get a glazed donut and a carton of milk. When I get home I write an e-mail to the Flans saying I won't make it tomorrow and will somebody else please bring salad. I feel relieved when I press "send." Then I feel sad.

That afternoon, once again, I am first in the car pool line. I crack open my book. Every once in a while I look into the rearview mirror and see the line of cars stretching out behind me. Three. Five. Ten. Twenty. Lisa must be somewhere back there, but I avoid getting out and looking for her. She'll give me shit for blowing off our Flan dinner. Or worse, she'll press that long-promised number of a therapist into my hand. Or maybe she'll play therapist herself. Sit in the car and ask me *Why are you here?* And I'll play dumb. *Here in line? Here in California?*

A Toyota Corolla pulls in front of me. I look up as the woman driving it backs up, so close to me our cars are nearly touching. For a second I am so stunned that I don't register what's going on.

Perhaps she just got a flat tire. Perhaps she dropped her cell phone and has to fish it out of the McDonald's wrapper detritus on the passenger seat floor before she continues on. When it becomes clear that she has no intention of moving, that she's just taken my rightful place in line, I begin giving her the dirtiest looks ever. Unfortunately she doesn't dare look again into the rearview mirror, which incenses me even more.

This kind of outright cheating, the blatant, brazen disregard for those already in line drives parents crazy. There is an order. It must be adhered to. I was told that on Ben's very first day of kindergarten. Above all else, do not try and cut in the car pool line.

I contemplate getting out of the car, marching up to her window and giving her hell. She slouches lower and lower in the seat, and for a moment I think she's StressErasing, too. I get a great view of what I must look like most days and decide right then and there I cannot StressErase anymore in the car pool line. I am on the verge of leaping out of the car, fantasies of our showdown flitting through my head, when our Car Pool Administrator, Kathleen, comes up the hill, walkie-talkie in hand.

I'll do the next best thing. I'll tell on her!

Kathleen walks up to the Toyota and leans in. A kind of Whoa! expression crosses her face and she backs away without saying anything. She comes to my car.

"Hi," she says. "Just Ben today?"

"That woman cut in line," I say. "There were fifty cars lined up and she just pulled in front of everyone."

Kathleen gives me a strange look. "She's weeping. I don't know what's going on, but she's weeping. She didn't even look up when I passed."

"She's *crying?*" I ask. "In the car pool line?"

Kathleen shrugs. "Have a nice day."

What's wrong?" says Ben a few minutes later when he climbs into the car.

"Nothing," I say.

"Did something happen?"

"Nothing happened."

"Then why does your face look like that?"

The woman in the Toyota Corolla is still there. She hasn't picked up her kid. I can't even see the top of her head anymore, that's how slouched she is in the seat.

I catch a glimpse of her shoulders heaving up and down and I can't help but imagine what has happened to her. What horrible news has she just received? Is her mother dying? Has her husband just informed her he's in love with somebody else? Did she miscarry? Is her house in foreclosure? Or is it something simpler? Has she just realized her life has not turned out to be what she expected it to be and is she now, right at this moment, laying some dream to rest? I wonder about all these things and at the same time I am selfishly thinking about my own safety. The well-being of my small family, intact for now—but tomorrow, who knows.

A wave of compassion and shame washes over me. That could be me. That could be any one of us. All of us sitting in our cars alone, day after day, year after year, waiting for those we love.

I think about what the young woman at the Mormon temple asked me. It occurs to me she was asking her question in capital letters—DO YOU KNOW WHERE YOU'RE GOING? Not today, not tomorrow, but after this life? I wish I were one of those people who knew where they were going next. I envy those people their faith, the sparkle and glitter of certainty. The best I can do is hope. I can say with all certainty that I hope I'm going someplace where all the people I love will be waiting for me.

"I'm sorry," I whisper to the woman as I pull out of the car pool line.

"Do you know her?" asks Ben.

"Yes," I say.

May

C AN I JUST READ YOU THIS TEXT?" ASKS TERRY.

I'm at the neighborhood swim club with some friends. The text Terry wants to share with us is from her new boyfriend.

"DLG, I can't believe 24 hrs have passed since I kissed U. 2-night can't come soon enough."

Terry looks down into her lap and sighs. Slightly forced smiles appear on the rest of our faces.

"What's DLG?" I ask, thinking it can't be Dirty Little Girl.

"Darling."

"Oh."

Now, as happy as we all are for Terry, and we really, really are, there's a brief pause in which all us are having our own private thoughts that are not safe to share. Such as:

- When was the last time I kissed my husband, I mean *really* kissed him?
- When was the last time I was desperate for him to come home? And not because the TiVo went on the fritz or there was a bat in the bathroom but because I felt lost without him?
- When was the last time *I* got a text like that? Never. I'm afraid of texting. Well, really what I'm afraid of is that I'll be sending a text and a teenager will come up to me and say you are far too old to be doing that. But perhaps we could do a trade? I could teach you how to not look like an imbecile texting and you could teach me how to memorize phone numbers.
- We have never called each other DLG. Ever, in our whole entire marriage. And what a lovely word that is. And so old-fashioned. How old is this boyfriend anyway?
- There's something wrong with my marriage. But I can't tell anybody. I have to just sit here and smile and be supportive and keep acting like a woman who says things like: You're going on a business trip? To Sweden? How wonderful. How I wish I could come. I've always wanted to go to the bear park in Orsa! But instead thinks things like: He's going for two weeks to Sweden? Yippee! I get the bed all to myself!

"That is so sweet," says Anne.

"Seems like a keeper," says Sue.

"My husband e-mails me little notes every morning, just checking in, have a good day sort of thing, but I don't write back," I say. "I read them but then I just delete them."

A woman I know walks by in a bikini. She's got one of those recently-divorced-yoga-hard bodies. We all watch her settle into her chaise lounge with her pile of magazines and books. We are fascinated and threatened. We envy her freedom, yet all that space scares us.

"Why did she get divorced?" asks Anne.

"I think her husband cheated on her," somebody says.

"And she divorced him?" says Anne. "Why would she divorce him over that? Everybody cheats, and if they don't cheat they want to. I mean at some point you have to say to yourself, *Who cares?* We're all ten or twenty pounds overweight and have another thirty years to go with each other. I say do what you have to do to go the distance."

"Hmmm," I say.

I suspect Anne has touched on something all of us who are in long-term relationships wonder at one point or another. How the hell are we going to stay married? Well, not just stay married, but stay *I can't believe it's been 24 hours since I kissed you* married. That is the question.

The next week my friend Alice comes to visit. Alice is ten years older than me and I've always looked up to her. She's mothered two wonderful kids. She's got a high-powered career and has been married for over thirty years. We've talked hormones and private schools, glasses and lip gloss. Now we've moved on to husbands.

I'm still in my confessional mode. "I'm a very neglectful wife. I hardly ever cook. My husband sends me notes every morning and most of the time I don't answer them," I tell her, expecting her to say no big deal, this is 2008, she doesn't cook or respond to e-mails either.

"You might want to start answering them," she says. "It hasn't happened to you yet, but it will; in a few years women will start eyeing your husband. It doesn't matter whether he's married or not. That won't stop them."

"But he drives around in that van."

"Some women love vans. Start being nice," she says. "And just so you know, it doesn't usually work in the other direction. Fifty-year-old men are not out there trying to steal away somebody's fifty-year-old wife."

"That is so sexist."

"It's the truth," she says.

When we get home I immediately send a little e-mail to my husband.

It's been 1,582 hours since we've kissed. Tonight can't come soon enough. Xxx, Me

He doesn't e-mail me back so I call him. "Did you get my e-mail?"

"Very funny," he says.

"It wasn't a joke. I was missing you."

Silence.

"No, I mean I was *missing* you," I say. "Maybe we should go on a camping trip."

"*You* want to go on a camping trip?"

"Well—kind of."

He snorts.

"No, really. Let's go camping. In the van."

"Hold on," he says.

I hear a woman's voice in the background and then the distant sound of my husband laughing.

"S'mores. Campfires. Boggle," I say.

"I'll have to call you back," he says and hangs up the phone.

These are dangerous times. It's hard not to feel unnerved when couples all around us are divorcing. In my experience things follow a predictable pattern after these couples have sorted things out with lawyers and custody. First they lose weight. Then they train to run marathons. Then they learn to tango. Then they get highlights. Then they tour the hill towns of Italy. Then they buy new, fabulous clothes and ask us if we'd like their old ones before they haul them off to the Salvation Army, and all along the way they have lots and lots of sex and make sure to tell those of us who are doing our best to stay married to the same person for fifty years all about it. *In detail.*

And because you don't want to seem like a prude, or for anybody to know that you go to bed at nine p.m., you agree to do crazy things with them like go to see the midnight showing of *Batman,* and then when the reality of what you've signed up to do hits you, you cancel at the last minute.

"Yeah, he came home from school with this sore throat. I think it's strep. *Cough. Cough.* I probably have it, too. I wouldn't want to give it to you, especially since you're having so much sex these days and having something like strep would really put a damper on that sort of thing."

Here are the facts: I have been with the same man for nearly twenty years. Even though I love my husband dearly, sometimes the reality of this is shocking. How did I get here?

* * *

Here's how I got here.

N.B. Jesus was my first love and pen pal. I offer as proof these journal entries. I have replaced the word "Jesus" with "Phil" so as not to offend anyone.

May 15, 1978

Phil, what a beautiful day! I am filled with love for you, Phil. I am yours. I am here to serve you. Just tell me what you want me to do and I'll do it. Just don't ask me to try out for track or eat lamb curry.

I see you everywhere, Phil—in the lilacs, in my Big Mac, in my new Famolares. Thank you, Phil, oh, thank you for this glorious day. And for all you've sacrificed for me. I can't wait to come see you in your kingdom. Well, actually, I can wait. Hopefully seventy years or so! Anyway, please, Phil, if I could just ask a little favor? If you could just see fit to do one little thing for me I would be forever in your debt. Could you send me a boyfriend? I really want to be kissed, and perhaps felt up. Please do not be insulted. You will always be first in my heart, Phil. But I'm fourteen now, and I want to have more, more, more joy in my heart, Phil, and in other places, too. So please, Phil, if you agree it is the right time— send me a boyfriend. Perhaps one named Kenny?

August 1979

Oh, Phil, thank you for sending me Kenny! I can't stop thinking about him. My heart and other places are bursting, bursting, bursting with joy. I understand, Phil, what you mean about heaven on earth, for surely this is heaven, the way I feel when I see him. When I see him see me. When we see each other. We are the kingdom and the kingdom is us.

P.S. Do not worry. We have pledged to not have sex until we get married.

July 1981

Oh, Phil, my heart and other places are broken, broken, broken as Kenny is now dating my twin sister, Dawn. How can this be happening? How can such sorrow exist in one person? I am so sad I can't feel you much anymore. I have been exiled from the kingdom and I am knocking at the door. Please, please, please let me in. If you have kicked me out because you think I have broken my promise about waiting to have sex until I get married, I need to tell you I didn't. You know, sometimes you have to go right up to the edge and it might look like you cross over, and maybe you stick a toe in but you don't go in, not all the way—do you get my meaning? Please, Phil, I have always loved you best. Forgive me and do not under any circumstances let Dawn into the kingdom. Hasn't she broken a commandment? Dating her twin sister's boyfriend? Shouldn't she be justly punished?

October 1984

Phil, thank you for sending me Rupert. He is a bit older than me. More sophisticated. For instance he tends bar. And has a mustache. And yesterday he took me to the gun range and taught me how to shoot an Uzi. Afterward we read Hemingway to each other and then we had sex. I'm sorry, Phil, I tried, but I couldn't wait until I got married. But may I remind you that all of us are your sons and daughters—even when we do bad things. We are all of us trying to make our way back to you. I'm very sorry to be so out of touch.

June 1989

Phil! Phil! Phil! This amazing man brought me to Singing Beach last night. We took the train from Boston to Manchester. I saw evidence of you everywhere I looked: in the lilacs, in our Amstel Lights, in his blue-green eyes. And when we stretched out on the sand, which was indeed singing (or squeaking), and he asked if he could kiss me and I said yes, in those seconds before our lips touched, you said, *Pay attention. This one. This one I made for you.* I haven't heard you that clearly since I was fourteen. Thank you, Phil. When I am with him nothing scares me.

* * *

I am taking Alice's advice and being nice. This is what I'm think-ing as my husband attempts to back the van into our campsite and I try to give him directions like a good wife should.

"Go left. Left. LEFT! Okay, I meant *my* left."

"You've got plenty of room. Two feet. Eighteen inches. Six inches. You should stop now."

"Yes, I know the difference between one inch and six inches."

"Why are you looking at me like that? It's a tiny scratch. Nobody can see it, unless of course you are looking for it."

"You want me to just sit here while you unpack? Are you sure? You would like some time alone in the van because you know where everything is and I know where nothing is? I'll go check out the bathroom situation. Don't forget to blow up my air mattress and set up the tent. I'll be sleeping in the van with you guys, but just in case. It'll be a great extra room, if anybody wants to take a nap or do a little reading."

Our campground is at Wright's Beach, which is on the Sonoma Coast, a breathtakingly beautiful fifty-three-mile stretch of coast-line famous for its cypress trees, fog, rugged headlands and long, sandy beaches. On my way to the bathroom I pass two signs that tell me of the hundreds of people who have died here, victims of rogue waves. DO NOT WALK PAST THE BERM and NEVER TURN YOUR BACK ON THE WATER, the signs advise.

I run back to our campsite.

"Where's Ben?" I ask my husband, who's inflating my air mattress. I cover my ears. "God, that's loud. Can't you close the van door? People are going to think we're vacuuming in here. What kind of people go camping and vacuum?"

My husband has the same look on his face he did when I was giving him directions on how to back into our campsite.

"Where's Ben?"

"On the beach."

"Unattended?"

"He's nine."

"I don't see him," I say.

"He's right over the berm."

I sprint out of the campsite and onto the beach. He is indeed right over the berm, not more than ten feet away. Apparently there are two berms—the berm (actually more like a lip of sand) that borders our campsite and the berm that slopes down to the treacherous water.

"Never, never turn your back on the water," I yell.

I reorient him so he's facing the Pacific, which is five hundred feet away.

"People have died here. Sleeper waves. Do you know what they are?"

He shakes his head.

"Waves that come out of nowhere," I say. "And just"—I wave my arm—"sweep you out to sea."

He looks at me blankly. "Did you find the bathroom?"

"I'm going now. Do you want to come?"

"No, thanks. I'll just go in the bushes."

"You mean the bushes right by the tent where I'll be sleeping?"

"I'll just go in the van," he says. "Like Dad."

"Dad didn't bring the Porta Potti."

"Oh," he says. "I don't have to go, then."

The worst thing about car camping is the bathroom and the fact that you have to share it with a hundred other people. I have been worrying about this for a week and have a good strategy in place.

1. Get up at five in the morning to beat everybody else to the bathroom.

2. Don't drink any coffee, or any beverage containing caffeine, thereby highly reducing the possibility of having to do nothing but pee for the next two days.

3. If desperate, use the bathroom at off-peak times like 3:22 in the afternoon.

"I told him about the waves," I say to my husband. "I'm off to the bathroom."

He nods. "I gotta hit the head, too."

And as he turns his back on me, unzips and pees into a bottle marked, WARNING: THIS IS *NOT* GATORADE, I think of the millions of other women who love camping, who love everything about it, who would be happy to be married to a man who had figured out how to stop making wasteful trips to the bathroom so he could do things like blow up his wife's air mattress instead.

An hour later our friends Kerri and Drew arrive. I am pleased to see they do their fair share of barking at each other, too, while getting situated. Setting up home, even a temporary home, is stressful.

"Don't put the tent up next to the bushes," instructs Kerri. "They smell like pee."

I give her a hug.

"Are the bathrooms disgusting?" she asks.

I look at my watch. "I'd go now if I were you."

We are all so curious, hungry for the truth. If only we could ask the questions we really want to ask of each other and get the real answers. Like how many times a month do you have sex? What prescription drugs are you on? Are you happy? Really happy? Happy enough?

I think about this as I look out at the aquamarine sea. I wish somebody could have told me the whole truth that long ago day on Singing Beach when my husband kissed me for the first time and some presence whispered in my ear that he was the one. That I would adore this man and at times I would hate him. That somebody would always want more and somebody would always want less. There would be days of boredom and irritation, days when life contracted and shrank and felt very, very small, but there would also be days of friendship, laughter and lust, when the world pushed us against its edges, when it nudged us somewhere new.

A kid walks by me dragging a kite, followed by another kid and another.

"Hey," I say, "you're walking through our campsite."

They ignore me.

"Did you see that?" I say to Drew.

Drew is a commander in the Coast Guard. I would like to be in an emergency with him. I'm dying to see him spring into action.

His hands are full with a paella pan. "What?"

"Those kids. They just walked right through our campsite."

"Well, there's probably not another way to get to the beach."

"Of course there's another way. Aren't there rules about that sort of thing? Campground etiquette? It's like a hotel room. This is our hotel room. Don't they know that?"

"Just tell them to walk around."

"You tell them. We're at the beach. This is your jurisdiction."

Half an hour later the same kids traipse back through our campsite.

"Commander," I shout.

He sticks his head out of the tent. "Walk around," he growls at the kids.

I imagine him on a boat, yelling into a bullhorn. *Prepare to be boarded.* I wonder what he looks like in his dress whites.

"Where's the TP?" he yells to Kerri and then I wonder no more.

In the afternoon we drive to another beach so the men can go surfing. Kerri, Ben and I set up our chairs by the van. We're too lazy to drag everything out to the sand.

"I'll be watching," I say to my husband, waving a pair of binoculars at him.

He usually surfs before work, so I never get a chance to see him in action. I know I need to make a bit of a fuss over him. Tell him how elegant and graceful he is riding the waves and how good he looks in his wet suit. And I would if only he didn't insist on donning a yellow helmet and ruining it all.

"They make helmets for surfing?" I say.

"You bought this for my birthday," he says.

"I did? Oh, right." This must have been one of those presents where he e-mailed me the link with a header that said *Thanks for the birthday present!*

I glance at the waves. "It looks pretty gentle. You probably don't need it today."

"I wear a helmet when I ski, I wear a helmet when I surf," he says.

"But nobody else is wearing a helmet. I mean, I'm so glad you are. To protect your brain and all. But don't people look at you funny?"

"I don't care what anybody else thinks," he says.

"I wish Drew would wear one," says Kerri.

"It's not really my style," says Drew, which is Coast Guard speak for *no fucking way.*

As much as I want to commend my husband for his safety protocol, I find it very hard to carry on a conversation with a straight face while he's wearing his headgear and I'm relieved when he and Drew tuck their surfboards under their arms and depart for the water.

"They should make tankini wet suits for men," notes Kerri, glancing at her husband. "A little mystery. That's what's needed."

It turns out I don't need the binoculars to watch my husband. All I have to do is look for his bobbing yellow head. I watch him catch a few waves, but then a young couple diverts my attention. He's surfing; she's scampering around on the sand and videotaping him. Every time he loses his surfboard (which is often) she jumps up and retrieves it, wades into the waves, hands it back to him and then they kiss. This makes me think of my old boyfriend Kenny, my first true love. He called me a couple of weeks ago and told me he was leaving his marriage.

"Are you sure?" I asked him. "Can't you go to couple's therapy? Try harder?"

"It's not a matter of trying harder," he said. "The truth is I lost myself. We lost each other. I don't know how it happened. But I don't think we can find our way back."

"Oh, Kenny," I said.

I could hear him three thousand miles away trying to choke back his sadness.

"For chrissakes," says Kerri, nudging me. "Are you seeing this?"

She points to the young woman running after her boyfriend's surfboard.

"How many times a month do you think they have sex?" I ask.

"Sixty," she says. "Possibly ninety. They've probably already done it twice today."

It strikes me that I used to be like this girl. Anticipating my husband's every need, worrying about his appetite and responding to every e-mail.

"Do you think we should go out on the beach?" I ask.

"No, just wave so they think we're paying attention."

We make a show of waving wildly and enthusiastically.

"Where's the Commander?"

Kerri shrugs. "They all look the same to me. Except for your husband, who looks like somebody cracked an egg yolk over his head."

An hour later they return. My husband peels off the top half of his wet suit and eats a granola bar but makes no move to take the helmet off. People walk by and stare at him.

"You're on dry land. You can take the helmet off now," I tell him.

He ignores me.

"No, really, it looks stupid," I say.

"I don't give a shit," he says.

"I wish I didn't give a shit," I say.

His face tightens and he rips off the helmet. "It's a fine example you're setting for Ben."

"You didn't need it. The waves weren't that big," I say.

"That's not the point. The point is to always wear it so you're prepared. And the waves can get big anytime. Especially here."

"Well, I was watching you. The whole time," I say in my defense, which is a lie. I watched him for five minutes, then I read my book. "You looked good out there."

He shakes his head.

"What? You want me to be like that girl?"

"What girl?"

"That girl on the beach who was watching her boyfriend's every move. Who jumped up to get his surfboard. Who ran into the sea to deliver it to him."

"I have no idea what you're talking about."

"I'm trying to protect you," I said. "So people don't make fun of you. That's our job. We're family. We protect one another."

"*People* aren't making fun of me. You are," he says.

I am not being nice. I am being the opposite of nice, but I can't seem to help myself. When we get back to the campground I retreat to my tent and proceed to spy on the group staying in the campsite across from ours. It's some sort of a reunion—aunts, uncles and cousins. Their campsite is cluttered with chairs, bikes, kites and three enormous tents and whenever they think we're not looking they walk through our campsite to get to the beach. The kids ride around on their scooters and shout "God Bless America," for some reason that I cannot fathom.

Meanwhile Kerri is making paella. She plays lacrosse with Ben and gin rummy with Drew. Every once in a while she comes to check on me. I fake sleeping the first time. The second time I bury my head in the pillow.

"Cheer up. Soon it will be dark and you can urinate on the beach," she says. "In the meantime we're playing bocce. Get your ass out here."

I have never played bocce before. It's a very simple game. You throw out a little yellow ball. Then you throw your ball at the little yellow ball. It turns out I am very good at bocce. I mean, really, really good. I jump around and whoop and do a fair bit of gloating.

"I think Mom's found her sport," says Ben.

After dinner I drag my chair next to my husband's and we stare out to sea like two widows.

"This is really easy for you," I say to him.

"What?"

"Camping. I really suck at it."

"Yes, you do," he says.

"I'm trying," I say.

"No, you're not," he says.

"I'm going to try."

He sighs.

"It's just that I hadn't found my sport, until now. Do you know what that does to a person? To have to go so long before finding their sport?"

"You're scared."

"I am not."

"You've always been scared, Mel."

"I'm sleeping in the tent tonight."

"I know. I put a lantern in there for you."

"Wanting to be comfortable is not the same thing as being scared," I say.

"Sometimes it is," he says.

The next morning Kerri and I take a walk on the beach. We make sure to stay high up on the berm, but to our surprise a few people are actually in the water. We wave our arms, signaling at them to get out, but they ignore us so we give up.

Before they moved to California, Kerri and Drew lived in Malmö, Sweden.

"That would never happen in Sweden," says Kerri. "People are so well behaved there. They follow the rules and not only do they line up for everything but they take a number. At first I thought everybody was really rude because they didn't make eye contact or say hello or smile or anything. But then I realized they were giving us our space. You could walk down the street in a bikini, or, say, that Van Halen T-shirt you're wearing and nobody would gawk. They wouldn't even look at you," she says.

"I forgot to bring a clean shirt," I say. "So I had to borrow one from my husband."

"That's the only shirt he had?"

"It's the only one he let me borrow."

We hike up a hillside and walk down a dirt road lined with wildflowers.

"Did you sleep well?" she asks.

"Heaven," I say.

"Drew farted in the middle of the night and it was so stinky it woke me up."

"Well, you're welcome to use my tent. I'm going to sleep in the van tonight."

"You are?" she says.

"Yes. Why is that such a surprise?"

We're almost back to the campground when a pickup truck drives past us. A man hangs his torso out the window, pumps his arm and yells, "Van Halen—woo-hoo!"

It's been a long time since I've been whooped at and we both stand there for a moment, shocked.

"Was he talking to me?"

"You're the only one wearing a Van Halen T-shirt," says Kerri.

"My husband did this on purpose. To punish me."

"Yes, I'm sure he did," says Kerri, laughing.

I would like to tell you that I keep my word, that I sleep in the van that night with my family, but when the time comes, as much as I want to, I can't bring myself to do it. Instead I crawl into my tent and spy some more on the huge family in the campsite across from ours. I feel like the little match girl. I watch them as they put their kids to bed. I listen to them cleaning up, washing the pots and pans, and stacking the bikes against one another. And then when it's dark, when the sky is studded with stars, the aunts and uncles metamorphose into brothers and sisters who drink tea, talk softly and poke at the embers in their campfire with sticks.

I think about how I have spent my life following directions, staying above the berm. I think about what none of us are willing to talk about. The rogue waves—the affairs, cancer, car accidents, mental illnesses—we know are lurking out there, waiting to sweep us out to sea. My husband is right. I am scared. But there's so much to be scared of because there's so much more at stake now. This life we have built together. Our son.

One of the last times I actually swam in the ocean we were in Hawaii. Ben was five. He was not water safe—he could barely do the crawl. I took him out and for a while things were fine. I held him in my arms and we bobbed around in the gentle swells. Then I made the mistake of turning my back on the water.

I heard the wave before I saw it and by the time I spun around it was too late. Nearly eight feet high, the wave crashed down upon us. Ben was torn out of my arms. And in that time which seemed interminable but was perhaps only twenty seconds or so, when I was pinned on the ocean floor and could do nothing but wait to see how badly I had fucked up—I thought please, *please, please, please, please, please*, don't let us be the unlucky ones.

My husband has since taught me that there's a safe place right under the churning white water. It doesn't matter how big the surf—in every wave there is a still point, a pocket of calm. To access that place all you have to do is dive under, precisely at the moment when everything inside of you is saying run, run! Trust in the safe place, he said, and the wave will pass right over you.

It seems to me that we're all allotted a number of perfect minutes, years if we're lucky, when everything is as it should be. When sleep comes without sleeping pills. When love is a birthright. When our houses are intact, safe from fire, mice and heartbreak. The thing I'm most afraid of is that those minutes are running out.

June

GUMMI BEARS AREN'T ALLOWED."

I grab a cart and wheel it into the drugstore.

"Skittles?" asks Ben.

I wave the list at him. "No candy of any sort. You need bug spray. Moleskin. Sunscreen. Band-Aids. And you're going to have to learn to wash your own hair. Your counselor is not going to do it for you. Just shut your eyes and keep rubbing your head until all the shampoo is out."

"How will I know when it's out?"

"When it squeaks," I say.

He looks at me bewildered but I pretend I don't notice. I'm a little mad at him for getting us into this predicament.

"You wanted to go to camp—I signed you up for camp. However, it's not too late to change your mind. I'll just say you got the flu. Do you feel a little sick? Light-headed?"

I feel like *I* have the flu. What was I thinking signing him up for sleep-away camp? He's only 111 months old. But back in January it sounded like a great idea.

"It's time for him to man up," I said to my husband. "Only children need to separate from their parents even more than kids with sibs. It'll be good for him to get away from us, and good for us to have a break."

"I don't need a break. I like having him around."

"Are you saying I don't like having him around?"

"I'm saying I think he's kind of young. It's going to be hard for you," says my husband.

"What do you mean? We'll be so busy. We'll go to concerts. I think the Indigo Girls are going to be in town. They always come in the summer."

My husband makes a face.

"Okay, we'll go out to see movies. Foreign movies. Movies with subtitles."

He makes another face.

"Okay, so I called my mother. She said he should go. It's important for his development."

My mother is a child-rearing expert. Her résumé includes having raised four daughters, running a psychiatric ward and being married to a pediatrician. It sounded so reasonable coming out of her mouth, so East Coast, so the mother I really want to be, a toss-him-in-and-see-if-he-floats kind of mother, but now that we are only a few days from dropping Ben off and I've read the camp literature more closely, I'm in a panic. It turns out I am more of a jump-in-with-him-strapped-to-my-belly-and-don't-let-him-out-of-my-sight-until-he-climbs-out-of-the-water-or-turns-thirty-whichever-comes-sooner kind of mother.

I am also a lazy mother. I should have done a little more research and gotten some referrals. This is not a high-end summer camp with Webcams and daily check-in calls from the camp administrator. It's a soccer camp up in the mountains that nobody seems to have heard of except for my friend Renee, who is also sending her only son, Parker.

But if cognitive behavioral therapy has taught me anything it's that I tend to skew toward the negative side of things. All that's needed is a little reframing and voilà! I'm in the midst of implementing a revolutionary child-rearing philosophy, weaning my son off his Best Life dependency and on to the Good Enough Life track.

Example: It's dinnertime. And your kid's 99 percent lean, humanely raised, nasturtium-fed hamburger is overcooked—the color of cardboard or a dead mouse. What's that you say? You can barely choke it down it's so dry? You'd like to toss it in the garbage and have me make you an organic Whole Foods hot dog, not an Oscar Mayer hot dog, and while I'm at it can I whip you up a side of black truffle risotto? Well, too bad, kid. Eat that burger. That burger is good enough.

I had not only convinced myself of the brilliance of signing my son up for a Good Enough camp but was feeling a little smug about it (and also fantasizing about how I could make millions by branding my Good Enough concept. It could apply to all sorts of things. There could be Good Enough college educations and Good Enough sex and Good Enough cars and Good Enough friends. It could be a whole new lifestyle, a movement!) until I read that I would not be allowed to communicate with my kid at the Good Enough camp unless there was some emergency. If I didn't hear anything, I should assume there was no emergency. If I got a call, then rest assured he would be in an ambulance on the way to the hospital an hour away.

This is what's driving my panic. There are so many other possibilities between no emergency and hospital, like homesickness and being bullied and sleeping next to a bunkmate who farts, talks in his sleep, or refuses to shower, that I am making myself crazy imagining them all.

"I'm going to camp," Ben says. "Stop trying to talk me out of it. I just wish I could bring candy. You told me that was one of the best parts of camp. Unlimited amounts of candy."

"Yes, well, I lied," I say. "This is not that kind of camp. Besides, you'll be too busy playing soccer five hours a day to think about candy."

"Five hours a day?"

He gives me that look again. The one that makes me want to lock him in the house forever.

"Okay, I'm exaggerating. Three. That's why you need the moleskin. For the blisters you'll be getting. From wearing your cleats from sunup to sundown."

I toss the Gummi Bears in the cart. "We'll hide them in your sleeping bag."

"But that's against the rules."

"Trust me. Everybody breaks the rules at camp," I say.

When we get home I go into my office, shut the door and call Renee.

"Don't forget to send the cards," I say.

"I put them in the mail today," she says.

"What did you write?"

"What's there to say? Score goals. I love you," she says.

"Is Parker excited?"

"Yes! So am I! I have so much planned. We're going to see Billy Joel. And *Chorus Line.* And out to dinner at Aureole."

"Wow, you're so organized. But isn't Aureole in New York City?"

"It is? Oh, what does it matter? It's our first week without him in nine years. The point is we have a lot to do. What about you guys?"

"Indigo Girls. *Mamma Mia!* Dinner at Breast," I say.

"There's a restaurant called Breast?" asks Renee.

"Yes, infants eat there all the time."

"This is going to be so much fun," she squeals.

"I know!" I squeal back.

I hang up and get out the cards I've bought for Ben. The Good Enough camp suggests that you put your letters into the mail days before your camper's arrival, thus ensuring they will arrive on time. I shudder as I search for a pen: what could be more traumatic than every camper but yours getting mail? The camp suggests you write calming, ordinary and reassuring things. I imagine such a letter:

Dear Son,

I'm sure you are having a wonderful time. Don't worry. You aren't missing anything here. *Star Wars XI* sucks. Take it from us. We've seen it three times! Occasionally (okay, every night) I've been sleeping in your bed (just to see what it's like to be you, not because I miss you so much that I want to puke) and I found out your mattress is full of bedbugs. Good thing you're at camp! I'm covered in bites, but don't you worry about that. I'm very sorry that I told you to buck up and stop being such a baby and perhaps hinted you might be a hypochondriac when you complained about being so itchy. Remember to floss and that afternoon is a good time to move your bowels. The bathroom will be far less crowded then.

I put my pen down. I'm feeling a bit nauseous. There's a knock on the door. My husband walks in. He looks at the card and then at my face.

"Do you want me to write it?" he asks.

I nod and hand it over. He quickly scrawls, Dear Ben, Hope you score lots of goals! Love, Dad.

"Stop moping," he says. "He's going to camp. Not the front line."

"Don't joke. There could very well be a draft by the time he's eighteen. The good news is that he's got my mother's feet."

"I don't think the Armenian flat-foot thing gets you out of the military anymore," says my husband.

I never thought of that. Should people with flat feet be playing soccer? He could be ruining his feet, stuffing them into those cleats.

"Take the afternoon off," says my husband, parsing the look of horror on my face. "I've got Ben. I'll do a man-up activity with him. Get him ready psychologically for camp."

This is what I love about being married.

"That'd be great," I say.

My husband looks at his watch. "Give us five, six hours. Don't come home before then."

"What are you going to do?" I ask. Now I'm worried.

"Trust me," he says. "It will be just what he needs."

When I return home that evening my husband and son are sitting quietly in the living room.

"How'd it go?" I say.

Ben glances up at me but says nothing.

"We had a great afternoon, didn't we, buddy?" says my husband. "We kicked the soccer ball around, then we went out for sushi and then we watched *Into the Wild,* that Sean Penn movie."

Ben nods.

"*Into the Wild*? That book about the kid in the Alaskan wilderness?" I faintly remember reading it years ago.

"Yeah. It's all about being true to yourself, right, bud? It's about possibility. And joy."

Ben shakes his head in agreement.

"It was a little long, but we watched the whole thing," my husband says. "I made him. I thought it was important. Especially the ending."

"Well, all right. Great," I say. "Into the wild we go! Camp will be a piece of cake compared to Alaska."

Late that night, when it becomes apparent that I won't be falling asleep anytime soon and my husband is in bed beside me, snoring and I'm fighting off the urge to punch him in the back, I watch *Into the Wild*. It's a stunning movie and for three-quarters of it I'm enthralled. I feel like it's talking directly to me, telling me just what I need to know. I find the parents in the movie a little annoying. Stop your whining and just let him go find himself, I think, and then I'm swept away by the amazing cinematography.

Oh, I love Sean Penn for making this movie. I love the rivers and the wheat fields and the forests. I even love the bus, until it becomes clear that the young man is about to die in it. How could I have forgotten how this book ends? Alexander Supertramp accidentally poisons himself and then starves to death very, very slowly.

I wake my husband up.

"You let Ben watch this?"

"It was good for him," he says.

"I can't believe you let him watch this."

"What?"

"He dies in the end. Violently. Alone. He starves to death and then goes crazy. How could that be good for him to see?"

"Can we talk about this later?"

My husband punches the pillow a few times, rolls away from me and within two minutes is snoring again.

In the morning I ask Ben if he liked the movie. He shrugs.

"What about the ending?" I ask.

He shrugs again.

"Did you understand what happened at the end?"

"He starves to death."

"Was that hard for you to watch?"

How could I have not been there with him? Explaining everything to him. Reassuring him this would never happen to him. I would never let him do a stupid thing like go out into the middle of the Alaskan wilderness with nothing but a sack of rice, a journal and a guidebook to edible plants.

"Actually it was kind of boring. I was pretending to watch but really I was playing my DS. I didn't want to hurt Dad's feelings.

Am I doing a good job of manning up?" he asks, stuffing his mouth full of French toast.

I wipe the corners of his mouth with a napkin. I picture him wandering around camp with a mouth encrusted with food.

"Yes," I say.

A few days later while we're in Lake Tahoe, spending the weekend at the Resort at Squaw Creek, a kind of last hurrah before we drop Ben off at camp, I die. At least my husband thinks I do. My last words, according to him are, "Oh God, oh God, oh God, not yet," and then I pitch forward onto his shoulder.

He sends Ben to get some water and then puts his ear to my mouth to see if I am still breathing. Then he spouts out a stream of nonsense: lyrics to a Green Day song, a list of shows we have TiVo-ed at home, movies we've yet to see. He doesn't know what else to do. I can hear him, and, although I can't respond, I find his recitation oddly comforting. It feels like he is talking me back from Jupiter with incantations of pop culture.

If one has to go, and we all have to go eventually—to camp, to the dentist, to the next world—there could not be a better way. Drift off while your husband whispers things in your ear like *Curb Your Enthusiasm* and *American Idiot* and *Live Free or Die Hard.* We should all be so lucky.

Obviously, I do not die. I faint from heat exhaustion because I am stupid enough to go for a run at an altitude of 6,000 feet a half hour after arriving in the mountains on a 100-degree day.

When I come to a few minutes later I am surrounded by people: my husband, Ben and Parker clutching Dixie cups full of water, an anesthesiologist and his nurse wife. Apparently I have caused quite a scene, slumped over as I am on a bale of fake hay outside a Ben & Jerry's, unconscious but with my eyes wide open (this detail provided to me gleefully by the boys).

The couple sits with me while my husband goes to get the car. The nurse takes my pulse and pronounces it a bit ragged but fine. I confess to the anesthesiologist that I love anesthesiologists, especially the one who gave me my epidural during the birth of my son. He says he gets this reaction quite a bit. I ask him if he would mind taking my pulse. He declines.

It is to be a weekend of firsts. Sending your kid away to camp or, in my case, watching my kid sprint away from me as fast as his legs will carry him to camp, is as big a moment as all the other firsts: walking, peeing in the toilet and cracking the code of the alphabet. A first for me—fainting in public. A first for Ben— seeing what his mother might look like dead.

But something is wrong. My experience is that some sort of emotion accompanies Ben's firsts, like a blast of fear or a trumpeting of anxiety—at the very least, a few sniffles. So, when the morning of his departure for camp finally arrives, I brace myself for all sorts of breakdowns: begging at the last minute to go back home, or pleading when he realizes that sleep-away camp really means sleeping in an eight-by-ten room with ten other stinky boys and no Nintendo, cartoons, or air conditioner for a week. Instead, he steadily and happily pulls away from me.

Finally, when I can't take it any longer, I ask if I can just have a little hug. He says he is too busy to hug me, so I remind him of the fainting incident. He shrugs and jumps into the pool.

"This is good," my husband says. "He needs to separate from you. He's too much of a mama's boy."

"This is good," Renee says. "He's compartmentalizing."

"This is not good," I say. "Tell me again what I said right before you thought I died."

One of my jobs, perhaps my most important job, is to educate my son. I don't mean to scholastically educate him—I leave that to his teachers. The education I'm talking about is much more ordinary but no less significant, and what every mother needs to teach her child: why Gummi Bears trump Skittles, why you should always sleep on the top bunk, why people are mean sometimes when they really want to be nice.

He breaks down, finally. Two hours before we drive him to camp, I hear him weeping in the shower. I run into the bathroom and peel back the shower curtain.

"I can't see!" he cries. "There's shampoo in my eyes. I'm blind!"

"Of course you can see," I say. "You're not blind. It's tearless shampoo."

"It's not tearless!"

"Yes, it is," I tell him. "It says so on the bottle."

I hold up the bottle to show him, and sure enough it reads "tearless." In fact, it is so tearless that it's called Baby, Don't Cry, but it seems this shampoo has the opposite effect, as my baby *is* crying. I wrap him up in a towel. I drape a cold washcloth on his head and let him watch *SpongeBob*.

A few hours later, he's gone.

Dear Parents,

If the phone keeps ringing and ringing and you are listening to this message for the tenth time and are wondering what the hell kind of camp this is that has nobody manning the phones, we would like to ask you to please calm down. It's only been twenty-five minutes since you dropped your child off and it's a beautiful drive back to the Bay Area. It's rare that you have four hours alone in the car with your husband and we suggest that you take advantage of this time and discuss things you couldn't normally discuss with your child sitting in the backseat.

Sincerely,

The Staff

"Well," says my husband, drumming his fingers on the steering wheel as we drive out of the mountains toward home, "our life with Ben is half over."

"Jesus, what kind of a thing is that to say?" I yell at him. "Do you want me to faint again?"

"Well, it's true. This is just the beginning of us dropping him off and leaving him places. Eight more years at home and then he's gone."

"Could we please talk about something else?"

"Okay. Did you get the Indigo Girls tickets?"

"Yes, for Wednesday night."

He's silent for a moment. "Do you think Renee might want to go with you?"

"You love the Indigo Girls!"

"Okay. I'll go. If you go to see *Batman* with me."

"What about that Mongolian movie? We need to do adult things. Things we wouldn't normally do because Ben's around. Six nights of freedom," I remind him.

I bite my lip. Why do six nights of freedom feel like six nights of imprisonment? Six nights that need to be filled before I can see my baby again and know that he's okay.

"It was really, really hard for me to leave him there. I felt like Sophie," I admit.

"Your Auntie Sophie? The hairdresser?"

"No, Meryl-Streep-Sophie. *Sophie's Choice,*" I say.

And because my husband is a kind man, he doesn't laugh at my comparing myself to a woman having to choose one of her children to send off to the gas chambers.

Monday morning I check in with Renee.

"This is Renee!" she sings into the phone.

"How are you holding up?" I ask.

"I'm great! I'm on my way out the door to get a pedicure and then acupuncture."

"You're not worried about them?"

"Not one bit," she says.

"Well, me either," I say. "This is going to be so good for Ben. I know it. It's just what he needs."

"Absolutely," she crows.

"They'll come back filled with confidence."

"And improved dribbling skills," she says. "Gotta go!"

Tuesday morning I check in with Renee again.

"This is Renee!"

"Hi, it's me. How are you holding up?"

"I'm fabulous. You know, it's the oddest thing. I don't miss him at all. I don't know why we didn't send them earlier. They could have gone when they were seven!"

"I wonder if they got our cards today," I say.

"Today, tomorrow. It doesn't matter. They're so busy and happy they probably don't even have time to open them."

I think about Ben's contraband Gummi Bears. He probably ate them all the first night and as a result got a huge stomachache. His counselor must know he broke the rules. I hope he isn't being punished. I should have put a package of wet wipes in his sleeping bag, too.

"Do you guys want to come to dinner with us tonight?"

"No thanks, I've got plans."

Tonight is game night, which means all sorts of fun games, like the This Is What It Would Feel Like If He Was Dead game, which entails wandering into Ben's room and picking up various pieces of soiled clothing and pressing them to my face and imagining he is dead, and the This Is What It Would Feel Like If He Was Gone to College game, which entails wandering into his room and picking up various pieces of soiled clothing with rubber gloves while holding my nose.

Dear Parents,

Please, we beg you, stop faxing us. We are aware of your child's peanut allergies, gluten sensitivities, blankie that must be hidden from all his other bunkmates until lights out at which point Counselor Ari will deliver it secretly under cover of darkness, bed-wetting (stress-induced), mild case of Tourette's (i.e., potty-mouth, i.e., fuck you I'm not playing goalie I am a striker, also stress-induced), constipation, nose picking and then sticking it on the bedpost compulsions. Yes, your son/daughter is wearing sunscreen and bug spray and yes, we force them to shower every day. Yes, with soap. Yes, we are administering their Ritalin, Adderall, Prozac, Allegra and fish oil capsules. No, we regret to inform you they are not their counselor's favorite. In fact, their counselor only pretends to like them and when they are asleep runs around the soccer fields wearing nothing but their size twelve Pull-Ups while smoking a joint. Parents, that was a joke. The Good Enough Camp has been operating for nearly forty years. Our point is we have seen everything. Nothing can surprise us. So please, please stop faxing us.

Sincerely,

The Staff

On Wednesday something shifts. I begin enjoying myself and barely think about Ben at all. I am not responsible for dropping anybody off or picking anybody up or asking anybody if they've brushed their teeth. I feel, well, I feel a little like Alexander Supertramp, in the good days, before he poisoned himself and began starving to death. I take a long hike. I write some nice sentences. I eat flan for lunch. In the evening my husband and I go to see the Indigo Girls at an outdoor amphitheater and we both get weepy when they play "Closer to Fine," which was the song that was on the radio the summer of 1989 when we first met.

We sing along. So does everybody else.

I'm trying to tell you something about my life.
Maybe give me insight between black and white

We rock back and forth and look up at the stars and let those sweet voices soak into us and we don't talk about our son. He's out there, somewhere, having a life without us, a life we can't track or know anything about. This is both terrifying and liberating.

Thursday morning I call Renee.

"This is Renee."

"Uh—Mike?" I say. She sounds like her husband.

"No, this is Renee," she says.

"Oh. Hi. You sounded kind of weird. The Indigo Girls were amazing!"

"I miss him so much," she confesses. "I've been sleeping in his bed. Don't you miss Ben? I think we should go tomorrow for the World Cup and pick them up."

"But they've got two more days. We're not supposed to pick them up until Saturday."

"Well, *officially*. But the counselor told me the semifinals for the World Cup are Friday night and we were welcome to come. Apparently a lot of parents do."

"But that's not in the literature. Are you sure?"

"I am not missing the World Cup," says Renee.

"Well, I'm not missing it either," I say. "We'll go together. The guys can meet us there on Saturday."

We are giddy on the drive back up to the mountains. It feels like Christmas morning.

"They are going to be so surprised," I say.

"Imagine their faces," says Renee.

We are so busy planning our surprise reunion that Renee plows through a small town going 50 mph in a 35 mph zone.

I see the cop on the side of the road. I see him crane his neck as we go by. He holds up a hand and I hold up a hand and wave thinking we must be a common sight: two mothers tearing down the highway to pick up their children at camp.

"I think that cop just gave me the peace sign," I say. "God, I love California."

"What cop?" says Renee.

A few seconds later he's chased us down.

"License and registration," says the cop, leaning in the window.

"Our kids are at camp." I lean over Renee to explain. "We're coming up early to surprise them. We were just so excited. You understand," I say.

He just looks at me.

"You've got kids?"

He looks at me again.

"Not that you look old enough to have kids. In fact, I'm sure you don't have kids. You look so young. Did you just graduate? From police school?" I ask.

He takes Renee's information and walks back to his car.

"Damn," says Renee.

"Maybe he'll give you a warning."

"Great idea." Renee sticks her head out the window and yells, "How about a warning? Sir? A warning?"

I stick my head out the other window and yell, "We promise we won't do it again. Please, Officer?"

"Do not get out of that car," he yells at us.

Once, when I was in my twenties and got stopped for speeding, the cop took one look at me and said, "Goddamn," and just walked away. Those days are clearly over.

"You're getting a big fat ticket," I say, leaning back in the seat.

Renee smiles. "It doesn't matter. It's my son's first World Cup." She reaches into the backseat. "Another Red Bull?"

*

We arrive a little early for the evening's festivities.

"Maybe we should kill some time before we go in. We don't want to be the first ones there," I suggest.

"We'll go to the snack bar and get a smoothie," says Renee. "Besides, I want to get good seats."

We pass a coach dressed all in blue. "Can I help you?" he asks.

"We're here for the World Cup," says Renee.

"Oh, yes, the World Cup. Well, that way, I guess," he says, pointing to the main field, his brow furrowed.

We continue on.

"I see flags. Do you see flags?" I say, trying to peer through the redwoods.

"Are those bagpipes I hear?" asks Renee.

I'm a little afraid Ben will have a heart attack when he sees me, so my plan is to get his attention from far away. Give a little wave. Then let it sink in that I'm here. Then give him a bigger wave. Then he'll run into my arms and I'll do my best not to sniff him to try to decipher exactly how long it's been since he's had a shower. I think that's Renee's plan, too, but we haven't discussed it.

We get our smoothies and sit down on the wooden stairs in front of the snack bar. Kids are drifting down from their cabins and milling about. I feel like my heart is going to rocket out of my chest. It's almost unbearable—the waiting. I have to fight my urge not to go tearing up to his cabin.

"Are we in the right place?" Renee asks after a while.

"It must be at a different field," I say.

"No, this is the right place, the flags are here."

Then our sons walk out onto the field and we both give a little groan of relief. They look so happy. Parker is giving Ben a piggy-back. Their socks are mismatched. Their hair is sticking up. Their mouths are rimmed Slurpee blue. They are fine, they are so fine without us and suddenly it hits Renee and me that we are the only parents who have come for the World Cup. The only parents so desperate to see their sons that they showed up a day early.

"Quick, hide," says Renee, ducking behind a bush.

I crouch behind her.

"We are hiding behind a bush," I say, and we begin laughing uncontrollably, so hard that we are bent over holding our stomachs.

"Oh my God, they're looking over here," she says. "Shut up, shut up, shut up!"

We freeze.

"He's going to recognize your legs," I whisper.

Renee's got great legs, muscular and tanned and well turned out in a pair of white shorts. But apparently muscular and tanned legs are not in short supply at the Good Enough Camp and Parker soon toddles away with Ben still on his back.

We wait until they're completely out of sight to make our run for it. And as we're jogging down the path Renee whispers, "Take it to your grave. We will never tell them we came early."

"Or that you got a $250 speeding ticket," I add.

We swear on it.

That night at dinner Renee says, "So the Indigo Girls were amazing?"

"Closer to Wine," I say, reaching for the bottle.

"We are ridiculous—the World Cup. I should have known," she says, rolling her eyes.

"It's not our fault. If we had sent them when they were seven we'd be old hands at this by now," I say. "We'd probably show up the day after camp was over."

"No, we broke the rules," she says.

"What rules?"

"The letting-your-kids-go rules. It would have embarrassed them so much if they had seen us."

"One day we'll tell them and they'll laugh. They'll think it's funny."

"When?"

"When they drop off their kids at camp and arrive a night early to pick them up."

Saturday morning we get there at just the right time. Not too early. Not too late. Adrenaline floods through me, but I force myself to stroll slowly up to Ben's cabin. He's standing out in front, dribbling a soccer ball.

"Hi, Ben," I say casually, trying to keep the emotion out of my voice. I don't want to embarrass him in front of the other boys.

We lock eyes and then he turns around and walks the other way. I stand there for a moment, stunned. Then I go after him.

"Hey, Ben." I grab him.

He looks at me blankly. I sweep him up and hug him.

"Hi, sweetheart. Hi," I say.

He's stiff and shows absolutely no emotion. When he sees his father, however, he flies into his arms, shrieking, "Dad!"

I try not to show I'm hurt, but I do a very poor job of it. I sulk through the World Cup and lunch. Ben keeps his distance, but when he thinks I'm not paying attention I catch him staring at me. When we get into the car he climbs into my lap.

"I was so confused. When I saw you it felt like you never left," he says. "I didn't know what day it was. I had been waiting so long for you to come get me and then suddenly you were there."

Once I heard a child-rearing expert say that "I see" was the only response you should ever give your children, if in fact you wanted them to reveal themselves to you.

"I see," I say.

"I didn't wash my hair. I lost my water shoes. I only brushed my teeth three times," he says.

"I see," I say again.

"I didn't eat the Gummi Bears," he says. He frowns. "I don't like Gummi Bears."

"You love Gummi Bears!"

"*You* love Gummi Bears," he says. "I love Skittles."

And so the conversation goes, all the way home. Ben asserting his independence—telling us that he is his own person with his own private life and we are not allowed anymore to decide what his favorite candy is or what he will be for Halloween.

The future stretches out in front of me. I see myself making more mistakes, not fewer. Holding on when I should be letting go. Letting go when I should be holding on. The first nine years were the easy ones—when I could, for the most part, protect him from everything; when I was always in the next room when he took a shower, ready to run in and rinse the soap out of his eyes.

"I've decided I don't want to be a comedian when I grow up anymore," he says. "It feels bad when you tell a joke and nobody laughs."

"It's a tough career. You have to have a thick skin," I say.

"I don't have a thick skin," he says after a while.

"Me neither," I say.

I turn my face away from him, thinking Oh God, oh God, oh God, not yet.

July

MARRIAGE CHANGES PASSION. SUDDENLY YOU'RE IN BED WITH A RELATIVE.

I can't remember who thought this saying up, but I'm sure it was a woman who was lying awake while her spouse snored loudly beside her.

This is not 1973, I remind myself. This is not some hotel in Chatham. You are not on your family's annual vacation to the Cape and this is not your sister lying next to you in the same bed, hogging all the blankets, breathing on you and periodically slamming her leg against the mattress so hard the entire bed shakes. No, this is your husband—the man that you love, the man that you voluntarily chose to spend the next one hundred years sleeping beside, which right now, at three in the morning, seems like a very bad choice, but what did you know? Who can predict these things? He slept like a dead person (and so did you) until your early thirties, at which point you stopped sleeping and he started driving his pigs to market in the middle of the night.

Snoring is just snoring. But there's a medical diagnosis for the twitching. PLMD—Periodic Limb Movement Disorder. As a result of my husband's snoring and PLMD I have developed IWTFKYD—I Want To Fucking Kill You Disorder. All my girlfriends have it. They may not admit it, but they do. It's a silent epidemic.

My sleep deprivation has only gotten worse in the past couple of years.

"Get used to it," my doctor said at my last checkup when I asked her for a prescription for Ambien.

"Forget the drugs. Get some earplugs. Men snore more when they get older and women sleep lighter. You're lucky he's too young for prostate problems. By the time he's fifty he'll be getting up two or three times a night. How old is your mattress? Maybe you need a new one. A firm mattress sometimes helps."

I think about this conversation as my husband's leg slams down on the bed again, so hard I am propelled out of my wife-sized hole, across the mattress and into his extra-large-husband-sized hole.

"Too hot," he says and pushes me away.

"We need a new mattress," I say, crawling back over to my side.

"Turn down the volume," he says.

"The TV's not on."

"What's that noise?"

He woke himself up with his snoring. If I weren't so tired I'd be laughing hysterically.

"We're getting a new mattress. Tomorrow," I say.

"Fine," he says.

"There's a name for your disorder. Would you like to know what it is?"

"I do not have a disorder," he says. "You have a disorder."

"If I have a disorder it's because of your disorder. Your disorder gave me a disorder."

He starts snoring again. I punch him in the back lightly. And then I punch him in the back a little harder. All this middle-of-the-night rage is really bad for a person. I have to do something about my IWTFKYD, or my marriage is doomed.

May I ask," says Steve at Sleep Galaxy, "a slightly personal question? What is the difference in weight between the two of you?"

"A hundred pounds give or take," says my husband.

"That's what I thought," says Steve. "I'm very good at guessing people's weight. What are you, about a buck eighty-five?"

"Close," says my husband.

Did Steve just wink at me? I'm glad this is a mattress store and not a ski rental hut where not disclosing my true weight is a matter of malfunctioning bindings and resulting torn anterior cruciate ligaments. Oh, the power of suggestion. If my husband is 185 that would make me—well—tiny. Tiny is a very good frame of mind to go shopping in, but I'm sure Steve knows that.

"Maybe we don't need a king," I say. "Maybe we could manage with a queen." For my fifth-grade-sized self.

"We're getting a king," says my husband.

"Memory foam," says Steve. "That's what I recommend for couples who have such a size differential. There's something for everybody in this bed." He looks at me. "Let me guess. The entire mattress shakes whenever he rolls over?"

How did he know?

He pulls down a dusty wineglass from a bookshelf. "Imagine this is filled." He places the glass on the mattress. "Now jump on it," he says.

"Oh, no, I couldn't," I say.

"Go ahead. Get on," he urges me. "Jump!"

I look at my husband. He shrugs. So I climb on the bed in my stocking feet and jump gently and then a little bit harder. I feel ridiculous doing this, but Steve makes his point; the wineglass goes nowhere. I climb off the mattress sheepishly.

"And for you," says Steve, looking at my husband, "what are you, about six-two—the most important thing is support. With memory foam you won't have any pressure points. People tell me it's like sleeping in a hand. Imagine. A giant's hand. Cupped. Like so."

He presses his hands together like he's holding a bird's nest.

"$2,000. Wow. That's some sticker shock. I guess that's what you get when you wait this long," says my husband.

"You're not alone. Some people come in, they haven't bought a new mattress for thirty years," says Steve. "Life is too short to not sleep well. And you folks have a lot of life ahead of you. How about I throw in two memory foam pillows for free so you can have the whole foam experience?"

You're getting a new mattress?" says Ben later that day. "Can I have your old one?"

"You don't want the old one. That piece of crap is going to the dump," says my husband. "Besides, your mattress is fine."

Ben makes a face. "It's just that I'm nine. And it's getting a little small for me."

"Get used to it. You'll be sleeping in it until you go to college," I say.

"Can I sleep in the new bed, too?" asks Ben.

"No," says my husband. "You have your own bed."

"Well, maybe just once," I say. "When you're out of town on business. He's curious. He's never slept on memory foam."

"*We've* never slept on memory foam," says my husband, rubbing his hands together, giving me the eye.

Do you smell that?" I ask my husband a few days later after we have settled in for our first night in our new bed.

Imagine a place. A place of nighttime renewal said the video on the memory foam Web site, which I've been visiting for days and can now recite by heart.

"What?"

"That odor," I say.

Where stress is relieved.

"I don't smell anything."

"It smells like rubber. Like gas. Like a kickball. And faintly like a cow field."

And what if you could go there? Tonight.

"I'm hot. Is it hot in here?" asks my husband.

"Don't sweat on the mattress. What if we have to return it? They won't take it back if it's stained."

And every night.

"Jesus, I think it's the mattress. It's breathing. It's conducting heat."

I leap out of bed.

"Where are you going?" he asks.

Wouldn't you want to go there?

"To get a plastic garbage bag."

"Why?"

178

"To put beneath you."

"I just paid two-thousand dollars for this mattress. I am not sleeping on a plastic bag."

I go into the kitchen and get the bag. I walk back into the bedroom. "Get up," I say. "I'll put it under the sheet. You'll hardly feel it."

"This is ridiculous," says my husband, trying to claw his way out of his memory foam hole. "This mattress is like quicksand."

Imagine a place of no sex. What if you could go to that place? Tonight and every night.

Steve does not seem surprised to see us.

"The memory foam is not for everybody, I'll give you that," he says. "It takes a while to get used to."

"It has this funny smell," I say.

"Oh, that smell?" he says. "It goes away, I'm told."

"You never told us it would smell."

He shrugs. "It's like cilantro. Some people think it tastes like soap. Some people love it."

"I think we need an ordinary mattress," says my husband. "A back-to-basics mattress. Something retro."

"How's this for retro? How about a mattress that has all the style and romance of Hollywood's most romantic era?" says Steve.

"That sounds like a little too much style for us," says my husband.

"It's called the Pureloom."

The mattress is edged in gold. It's nearly sixteen inches thick. It's covered with the plushest of pillow-tops.

"No," my husband says.

"Handcrafted," Steve says. "Go ahead. Get on."

"No," says my husband again.

I lie down on the mattress and groan.

"Damn," says my husband.

"I'll give you guys a few minutes," says Steve.

"Just try it," I say.

My husband rolls his eyes and gets on. Then he tucks his hand between his knees and falls asleep. Fifteen minutes later I go find Steve.

"How much more?"

"A few hundred."

"How many more hundred?"

"Ten hundred."

"A thousand!"

"You'll have this bed for life. It's the kind of bed you hand down to your children. Trust me."

I give him my credit card.

I do not tell my husband we've spent $3,000 on this mattress. I keep it to myself, but by the time we get home the price seems obscene and I think I should cancel the order. I call my friend Robin for some advice.

"I just spent $3,000 on a mattress," I say. "I should return it, right?"

"That depends. Does the mattress have a name?"

"Allessandra," I say.

She sighs. "Allessandra. That's so exotic. Ours is probably called Ira. Is it amazing?"

"I've never felt anything like it."

"Then keep it. You're going to spend a third of every day on that mattress. Can I come visit Allessandra?"

"Yes. She'll be here tomorrow."

"Let me know once she's settled in and I'll pop by for a quick nap. I'd offer up Ira's services, but he's a nebbishy little thing."

"I'm so excited," I say. "I know this is ridiculous, but I feel like it's the beginning of a new life. For us both!"

I never knew it could be like this," I say to my husband a few days later as we are preparing for bed. "I'm happy. I'm so happy."

I've been sleeping all night long. I barely hear his snoring. In fact, I think he's stopped snoring. It's a miracle.

"It's too bad we can't see the headboard anymore," says my husband. "The curly maple headboard that my oldest friend handcrafted just for us for our tenth wedding anniversary."

"You can see it—just press down on the mattress. There. Like that. A whole three inches is exposed. Give me a hand, will you?"

He hauls me up on the bed. "You need a stepstool."

I haven't told my husband, but I'm having an affair with our mattress. I think about her all day long. Anytime I get a chance I go visit her. The first thing I do is strip her of her sheets. I prefer to see her undressed, in her natural form. The way I first saw her in the mattress store. That's how she is best appreciated. Her thoroughbred lines. Her Belgian jersey knit, hand-tied pillow-top.

I'm going to have to be careful. There have been a few times when my husband has caught me trying to sneak off to bed at seven.

"Don't disappear. We have things to do," he says.

"Like what?"

"Bills and weeding and what about that back rub you promised me?"

"I'll give it to you on the bed," I tell him.

"No, thank you," he says. "I would like it here. On the floor. By the way, I've been asked to go to Singapore. I'll be gone for two weeks. Do you want to come? You said you always wanted to see the East."

"Two weeks is a very quick trip to Singapore. You're barely over the jet lag and then you have to come back. I think I'll just stay here. Hold the fort," I say, while inside I'm thinking, Holy crap! I get the bed all to myself for fourteen nights.

Space. I crave it. I have only one child and one husband, but still, it feels like such a limited and precious commodity.

The first night my husband is gone, Ben grabs his pillow and crawls into my bed.

"What are you doing?" I ask him.

"I'm sleeping with you tonight."

"You most certainly are not," I say.

"You said I could," he says. "When Daddy went on a business trip."

"I did?"

"Yes," he says.

"Look," I say. "We are not a family bed kind of family. Besides, you kick."

"I don't kick. Anymore."

"Yes, you do."

"Fine," he huffs and rolls out of bed.

"Sleep tight," I yell to him as he trudges down the hall.

While my husband is in Singapore I stretch out into that bed. I live into it. I *dream*. I know this kind of dreaming is dangerous. I am not fantasizing about being with another man but about having my own bed for the rest of my life. Does this count as cheating? Who cares? I feel like I'm on my honeymoon.

But all too soon the honeymoon is over. Once my husband returns home he mentions something about a crick in his neck. Then he asks if his constant snoring is bothering me.

Then he asks if I would mind if he put a piece of plywood beneath the mattress, on just his side. Then he asks if it's possible to beat the pillow-top off a mattress with a broom. Just bat it down a little bit so it's not quite so soft.

And then one morning he says, very quietly, "I know you love this mattress, but I hate it. I haven't had one good's night sleep since we got it. I'm really sorry, but we have to return it."

The problem is we are past the thirty-day comfort guarantee, which as far as I'm concerned is a great problem to have because we are not returning this mattress.

We go back to Sleep Galaxy. Steve pretends he's never seen us.

"Hey, folks. What can I do for you today?"

"Remember us?" says my husband.

"No, sir. Should I?"

"We bought the memory foam bed and returned it and then we bought the Pureloom?"

"Oh, yes, about a year ago?"

"A little over a month ago," says my husband. "I know it's past your thirty-day comfort guarantee window, but the bed's not working out for us."

"I'm very sorry to hear that," says Steve. "But there's not anything I can do about it. It's been too long."

"See?" I say to my husband. "We can't return it. Let's go home."

"What a shame. That bed *is* an heirloom," says Steve.

"That's what I've been trying to tell him," I say.

Steve nods and glances up at Ben, who's running around the store trying out different mattresses. His technique is to jump on them and then fall down in a heap and pretend to snore. "I have an idea. Perhaps you can pass it down to your son and you folks can get a new one."

I gasp. "The Allesandra? But he's nine."

"Steve's right," says my husband. "I've thought about it and it's the only thing to do. Give Ben the mattress and we'll get a new one."

"That mattress cost three-thousand dollars," I whisper to him.

"I thought you told me it was an equal trade."

"Almost equal, but there was delivery and taxes," I say. "They add up."

He shakes his head. "He'll grow into it."

"It's obscene. No nine-year-old boy should sleep in a king-sized bed."

My husband shrugs. "It's the only solution. Steve, we need a mattress with absolutely no pillow-top."

"There are no beds with no pillow-tops," says Steve.

"None? Are you sure?"

"Well, maybe one," says Steve.

It's a slab. A Fred Flintstone bed. It's delivered the next day.

"Where do you want me to put this?" asks the delivery guy, propping my beloved Allessandra against the bedroom wall.

"In there." I point to Ben's room.

"Really," says the delivery guy, eyeing the Pokémon posters and the Star Wars plastic light sabers scattered on the carpet. "I'm not sure it will fit."

"It'll fit."

"Just barely," he grunts.

When Ben gets home from school he says, "Did the mattress guys come?"

"Yes," I tell him.

He squeals and runs into his room. He rolls all over the bed, marking it. "I can't believe this is mine! I can't believe it! It's so big. I'm so lucky. What are my friends going to say? It's like sleeping on a country. On all of Europe."

I can't believe it either. I'm trying very hard not to cry. Down the hallway I can see my future. The sliver of the mattress that I will be sleeping on for the next twenty years. And I hate my husband. I *hate* him.

"I can't believe you've done this to me," I tell him that night. "That you're making me sleep on this board."

"Sleep with *me*," calls Ben from his bedroom. "The bed's big enough for both of us."

"She's not sleeping with you, she's sleeping with me," yells my husband.

"I'm not sleeping with either of you," I say, getting out of bed and going to the guest room, where I proceed to lie awake all night long.

I can't get Ben's words out of my mind. They're jarring, coming from a child's lips—innocent, of course, but there's also an insistence, an entitlement behind his request for intimacy. The truth is that often I do things with my son that I used to do with my husband. Why? Because it's easier—nothing is required of me in return. We sit on the couch together, curled into one another like puppies. We eat ice cream from the same spoon. I listen to what he says, intently, as if every word is a poem. I used to listen to my husband that way. Why don't I do that anymore? What am I afraid of? That there's not enough love? That I will run out?

It's a slippery slope. I sleep in the guest room tonight. And then I sleep in the guest room tomorrow night. And the night after. And the night after. And pretty soon we're officially sleeping in separate beds. I will tell myself when something bad happens that I'll go back into our bed. We'll come back to the *us* that we used to be, back when we knew that no matter what happened, no matter how bad it got—if we both lost our jobs, and one of us got sick, and there was famine or flood or pestilence, or God forbid, something terrible happened to Ben—we still had each other. Life might strike us down, but we'd go on. Yes, that's what's going on. I've been squirreling away my love for the day when I'll really need it.

But here's the thing. The day when I really need it will be when it's too late, the existential kind of too late, and on that day I know I'll be doing something stupid, like xeroxing my taxes and I'll be doing something even stupider, like xeroxing them at my office in San Francisco (a bridge away from home) because my toner's magenta cartridge will have run out of ink and I will have refused to spend the $90 to remedy the situation just on principle. I am not the kind of person who prints in pink. Why should I pay for magenta?

One of my friends will run into my office screaming something along the lines of: "We only have thirty-two minutes left! Go find your family and get the hell out!"

Studies show that in a disaster we humans do one of three things: flee, fight, or freeze. I'm quite certain I will flee. It won't occur to me to question why thirty-two minutes or how anybody could know so precisely when the end is coming. I will just get in my car and like millions of others try and make my way over the bridge and home.

Traffic will flow nicely for a while and then it will just stop. I will drum my hands on the steering wheel and try not to be upset. But the waste! I won't be able to stop thinking about the waste. All my preparations for naught!

At home I will have three closets, each designated for a different disaster. The closet in the guest room will be for terrorist attacks. Besides twenty gallons of water and three quarts of bleach, there will be rolls of plastic sheeting and duct tape and a fake gun in case the terrorists come door-to-door.

In the office will be the closet for avian bird flu. On these shelves I'll have contraband Tamiflu I ordered from Canada, ten boxes of Kleenex, lots of disposable bags for puke and hundreds of rolls of toilet paper for diarrhea.

In the laundry room will be the closet that contains the earthquake supplies. In here will be a solar-powered radio, coils of mountaineering rope, carabiners, headlamps, a pickax, $1,000 in small bills and three boxes of white wine.

Thirty-two minutes. What can you do in thirty-two minutes? Wash a load of whites? Bleach your teeth?

I'll get out of my car when I realize I'm going nowhere. So will everybody else on the bridge. It will be like those disaster movies where tragedy strikes so quickly that a sort of preternatural calm descends upon everybody and everything. Nobody will scream. Not one person.

How will the world end? Will it be an earthquake? Will it be an asteroid? A nuclear bomb? Or will the universe buckle and fold? Will something just nail it? Bring it to its knees? I can only report how I'd like the world to end and you'll have to draw your own conclusions.

The blue will begin dribbling down from the sky as if someone were pouring it out of a pitcher.

"You, hold my hand," an elderly woman who has just stepped out of a Mercedes will say to me.

"No, thank you," I'll tell her. I am from Rhode Island. I don't touch people I don't know.

"Do you have children?" she will ask.

"Yes, a son."

"A husband?"

I will nod.

"Hold my hands," she'll say. "Pretend I'm your husband and your son and I'll pretend you're my mother."

I will cry then, but softly so nobody will hear it. My baby. Alone. Crouched under his desk, his head cradled in his arms. Having memorized all those multiplication tables and state capitals for nothing. And my husband. In his van. On the bridge, just a few hundred cars behind me, a mere quarter mile away, but I will never know how close he was because that's just the way it works in these kinds of scenarios.

"Don't," the woman will say. "You'll see them soon."

And I'll believe her. What else can I do?

We'll hold hands. We'll look up into the sky. It will smell grape, like Sweet Tarts.

A few seconds later it will lap us up.

I have something to tell you," says my husband the next night. "This mattress is too hard. It's too hard even for me. We have to return it. I'm very sorry I put you through this."

"You can't be serious," I say.

He nods. "I'm afraid I am."

There's only one thing to do. We drag our old futon, our first shared bed, out of the closet. We slept on this bed when we had nothing. Before ACL injuries and age-related shoulder impingements, when we ran five miles a day just for fun, just because we could and it felt good.

"Do you know you never snored when I first met you?" I say as we are putting on the sheets.

"I snored," he says. "We were just drunk all the time so you didn't notice."

"We weren't drunk *all* the time."

"We drank a lot. Every night. It was the nineties. Everybody did."

"Those were the days."

"Should I get you a glass of wine?" he asks. "A shot of tequila?"

I look at my husband and I see him. I mean I *really* see him. Something falls away, and all the men he's been in the years I've known him pulse beneath the surface of his face: the twenty-four-year-old who so staggered me with his animal grace, the thirty-three-year-old father tenderly cupping the head of his newborn son, the forty-year-old who taught himself to surf because he needed a new challenge, he needed a religion.

You act like a woman in love. You become a woman in love. I don't know who said that, but I believe it with all my heart.

"How about a piece of that blueberry pie?" I say. "One spoon."

August

YOU GO FIRST," I WHISPER TO BEN. "AND TRY AND ACT NORMAL."

He hesitates and I give him a little shove and he scampers through the metal detector, looking both terribly guilty and terrified, as if he's about to be zapped with 1,000 volts of electricity.

"Phew," he says, having made it through.

He would make a very bad drug mule.

"Next," says the security agent, motioning to me.

I walk forward, trying not to betray my nervousness, for in my carry-on bag, which is being x-rayed right at this moment, is a gallon-size plastic bag full of white powder.

I watch as the screener stops the belt. She screws up her face as she turns the image of my bag from left to right, trying to figure out what the hell is in there.

"Put your shoes on," I say to Ben.

The screener motions to her coworker. They both stare at the image. Then they stare at me. I fold Ben protectively in front of my chest.

"You told me to put on my shoes," he says.

"Quiet," I hiss.

"Okay, so you're wondering what that bag of white powder is," I say to the screeners. "I don't blame you. I know it looks suspicious. I would wonder, too."

The line of people behind me takes a collective step back.

"Shit," I hear somebody say. "I'm going to miss my plane."

"It's my dog," I say loudly.

The screeners look at me like I'm crazy.

"My dog in the Ziploc baggie. His ashes."

One of the screeners shudders. "I'm very sorry for your loss, ma'am," she says and starts the belt again, waving the line on.

"It happened a while ago," I say. "Last December."

"That's not very long ago," the screener says, looking at Ben, her face softening.

"No, it's not," I say, wondering what this can buy me. Early boarding? An extra cookie?

"Heel," whispers Ben to my carry-on bag as we make our way to the gate.

"I'm so sorry," says a man who was behind us in line.

"On your left," says his wife, pushing past us.

"That's okay. We're okay," I say, moving out of the way.

A few hours later, somewhere over Colorado when I'm half asleep, I hear Ben telling the flight attendant, "My dog died."

"Oh, sweetie." She squats by the seat.

He nods sadly. "He's under the seat." He kicks my carry-on bag. "In a baggie. Would you like to see him?"

"Ben," I reprimand him. "I'm sorry," I say to the flight attendant.

"Oh, no, that's okay," she says, her gaze flitting to the front of the plane. "Let me see if there's something I can do. To make you more comfortable."

She scurries down the aisle and I sit up. Properly. Formally. Trying to look like somebody who belongs in first class.

"Put your shoes on," I tell Ben.

"Why?"

"I think she's going to see if there are any seats in first class," I whisper.

I jam my feet back into my sneakers.

"We're going to sit in first class? I've never sat in first class!" Ben yells.

"Shhh," I say, looking around furtively. "People don't want to know about your good fortune."

"What if there's only one seat?" he says. He gives me a worried look. "I guess I'd be okay up there all alone."

The attendant walks briskly back toward us.

"Here you go," she crows, handing Ben a pair of plastic captain's wings. "These are from the flight deck. For bravery," she says. "And a pillow and a blanket," she hands them to me. "To make Mother more comfortable."

"That's so thoughtful," says Mother. "May I ask you a question? Do you think there's any chance we—"

"My dog died a few years ago," the flight attendant stage-whispers over Ben's head. "He ate rat poison. Poof. Gone like that."

I nod empathetically. We're now officially members of the Dead Dog Club. Everybody has a dead dog story, and once your dog dies they want to share it with you, kind of like everybody has a birth story and once you get pregnant you are required to hear all the details of your friend's protracted labor and how long she pushed and the drugs she took or didn't take and how her partner was e-mailing on his BlackBerry right up to the very last moment the baby was crowning and your friend screamed at him to get off his goddamn phone or she'd stick the phone so far up his butt that the doctor would have to suction it out with a vacuum.

"What was your dog's name, honey?" the flight attendant asks.

"Bodhi," says Ben.

"Oh, like in that Patrick Swayze movie?"

"Exactly," I say.

"No, like in Buddhism," says Ben, giving me a dirty look. "The Bodhisattva. The enlightened one?"

"Wow, smart kid," she says, after a beat, and then hightails it out of there.

We are on our way to Maine for our annual summer vacation. Our first stop is Freeport. This is where my younger sister, Sara, lives. It's also where I used to live right before we moved to California. In short, Sara is living the life I thought I would have, but she's living it so much better than I ever could, with a huge backyard, a mosquito zapper, a kayak, three children, and the quaint Bow Street Market directly across the street from her house.

Sara really has the Maine life down. For instance, she takes full advantage of L.L. Bean, the flagship store of the Freeport outlets. When I was living in Maine I did not know you could have playdates there. I did not know that in fact, playdates were encouraged.

It made sense. Where else were you going to go during the eight months of winter? Also they have convenient mothers' hours, as they are open twenty-four hours a day.

Sara might call one of her friends and say, "Hey, meet me at Bean's, in Tents and Shelters at 5:34 a.m."

Her friend might say, "We did Tents and Shelters yesterday. The kids are Tented and Sheltered out. How about Gear and Tackle?"

Sara might say: "Gear and Tackle has an age requirement of eight. I can meet you on the stairs in front of the stuffed beaver, or in the elevator. How about a playdate in the elevator?"

Besides being family-friendly, L.L. Bean's also has the best return policy of any store in the world. You can even return stuff you never bought there.

"Um, sir, I'd like to return this pocket flashlight."

"Certainly, madam. Were you not satisfied?"

"No, I was not satisfied. My three-year-old put it in a cereal bowl, poured milk over it and sprinkled it with sugar and it wouldn't work after that."

"I'm sorry, madam. And when was this?"

"This was—well, it must have been—1976."

"Oh, welcome back, madam! Welcome back! Very well, here is your money. We are giving it to you with adjustments made for inflation and 2008 pricing and emotional distress. That's ninety-nine dollars and seventy-five cents. Would you like that in cash? I am very sorry the pocket flashlight did not live up to your expectations. And is this cute little tyke your grandson? Did you know we have a playdate program here? No, I would not come between five and six a.m. It gets very crowded, especially in Tents and Shelters. The mothers tend to sleep in the tents, while the children pee on them. What's the little tyke's name? Oh, a fine name. May I give you a tip? Do not bring little Achilles to Archery. In fact, avoid Scopes and Rangefinders, too. May I suggest Water Fowl?"

It's late in the afternoon when we arrive at Sara's. She greets us at the door holding nine-month-old Josie in her arms. Her boys, five-year-old Julian and three-year-old Alek, peer through her legs shyly. It's been a year since we've seen them.

"Oh my God, you're here," she says and immediately we both start crying.

I have never met Josie. I've only seen pictures. I flap my hands enthusiastically and Sara hands her over. She makes dolphin sounds and smells of pears. I'm instantly in love.

"Julian," says Sara, "show Auntie Mel and Ben your new glasses. You know Auntie Mel wore glasses? From the time she was in second grade."

"Yes, that's true," I confirm. "I am basically blind. But you're not blind. You're just a little nearsighted, right?"

"Farsighted. We had no idea he couldn't see," Sara whispers to me.

That's what my parents said about me, too. Turns out I wasn't lazy and not living up to my potential. I was just lazy.

Julian steps forward wearing navy blue glasses that magnify his eyes so they look enormous.

"How many fingers?" says Ben, holding up his hand.

"Eighty-two," says Julian. "What's in the bag?" he asks, pointing to my carry-on.

Of course, he's looking for his present, which I haven't bought yet. I am the kind of auntie who buys presents in the local drugstore of the niece or nephew who is expecting the present.

"Bodhi," says Ben.

"Bodhi the D-O-G," says Sara, looking horrified.

"Yes, the D-O-G," I spell it out, too. "He D-I-E-D and we've brought him home to B-U-R-Y-H-I-M."

"J-E-S-U-S, that's horrible. Ben, I'm so sorry," says Sara.

"I don't think you have to spell Jesus. When somebody Jewish says Jesus she's not swearing, right?" I ask. "Because Jesus is not your lord and savior so you're not taking his name in vain."

Sara sighs. Back when she got married she and her husband struck a deal that I'm sure seemed eminently doable in the throes of new love. She would convert to Judaism and in return he would take her last name. He followed through on his part of the bargain, but seeing as they hosted Christmas at their house last year I'm not so sure how she's holding up on hers.

"So it's just the two of you? No husband?" Sara asks.

"He'll be coming in a week," I say.

"Great, we'll have some girl time," she says. "Ben, you've had a very long day. Would you like some granola? It just came out of the oven."

Ben follows her into the kitchen, a look of wonder on his face as if he's just wandered into a fairy tale. I know exactly what's going through his head. *Why can't I live here—in a house where mothers make homemade granola and children awake rested and happy from afternoon naps?*

"I used to make you granola," I say to him.

"You did? I don't remember that."

"Well, nobody remembers anything from when they were two."

The great thing about sisters is you can look at their lives and imagine this could have been you if you had just made different choices. Lived in a different city. Had a little more of the mother gene. Stuck it out in gymnastics, or finished *War and Peace.*

I watch Sara bustling around the kitchen while her infant daughter sits on the rug at her feet and babbles happily and her sons chase one another around the dining room table. I know how Ben feels because I feel the same way. We are both wondering *Is this what a normal family looks like?*

Maybe this is what every woman does when in the presence of another family. She rates her happiness, her irritations—the richness of her life—her joy. And she thinks about children or the lack thereof. Did zero turn out to be the perfect number? Or two, or three, or four? Do those with one wish they had two? Do those with two secretly wish they had stopped at one? All I know is that when I play this game I always come up with the wrong number. I suspect I am not alone in this.

Before dinner, Julian and I have some quiet nephew/auntie time on the couch. Because I haven't seen him for a year we have to get to know each other all over again, and this is tricky. Julian is no pushover. He's a typical oldest child—he makes you work for it. I've taken out my contacts because they were bothering me and put on my glasses.

"We're twins," I say to him, trying to find some common ground. "Look at us. Two four-eyes."

He stares at me intently, then kicks my ankle.

"Please don't kick my ankle," I say.

Last summer was the summer of *Please don't spit on me, people don't appreciate it when you spit on them, stop spitting, stop spitting on me now, goddamn it! Oops, look at that, I accidentally spit on you while I was yelling. How does it feel to get spat on? Isn't this a fun game? A fun, secret game that we should never tell Mommy or Daddy about? Oh, don't cry. Why are you crying? Sara, I have no idea why*

Julian's crying. I think he's hungry. Why don't you give him some of that fine granola that you just made?

I'm really hoping Julian doesn't remember last summer. Perhaps he couldn't see me back then. Perhaps I was just a blur and the reason he spat at me was to distinguish between my being a person or a rocking chair. Better yet, maybe he thought I was Auntie Dawn. Yes, that was it. Auntie Dawn was the aunt who spat on him.

"So what's it like having a baby sister?" I ask. "Is it just so much fun?"

He spits on me and runs from the room.

"Did he just spit on you?" says Sara, coming into the room.

"I'm sure it was an accident," I say.

"Josie is a touchy subject," she says, handing me a dish towel. "It's been quite an adjustment. I have to watch the boys every minute. A week ago I caught Alek trying to smother her with a pillow."

"Is that normal?" I ask, for the moment feeling very sure that one child is the right number.

"Apparently so. I asked Mom. She said the three of you used to try and murder each other all the time. Dawn in particular. She was a biter."

"And a spitter," I say.

"Really? That must be where Julian gets it from."

"She probably taught him. They probably played spitting games," I say. "Last summer, for instance."

We hear Josie scream, a thud and then the pitter-patter of small footsteps fleeing the scene of the crime.

"Alek!" hollers Sara and runs off.

Saved by Alek—that little troublemaker. How I love middle

children: their slyness, their deviousness—their charm. I am a middle child, well, sort of, if you count Dawn and me as one. What people don't understand about middle children is that when you've got no standing to lose you are free.

At 5:30 sharp we carry bowls of corn, salad and pasta outside on the deck. I feel a little bit stoned, having spent the afternoon playing Sorry and reading *Ferdinand the Bull,* all the time knowing exactly what lies ahead—bedtime at seven and waffles in the morning. I could be another child in Sara's house. I could relinquish everything to her and it would just be taken care of.

"I would like to be your kid," I tell her, which is a strange thing to say because Sara is eight years younger than me. "You could adopt me," I say.

"Or you could move back to Freeport," she says.

Sara's husband, whom I adore, who happens to have the same first name as my son and my husband and the same last name as me (it's confusing, so mostly I call him Hey) brings me a beer and some mosquito repellant.

"Don't you miss Maine?" he asks.

"Desperately," I say, as I spray myself head to toe with Off.

"We got a new zapper," he says. "Don't overdo it."

The zapping sound is straight from my childhood; it's the sound of the New England suburbs circa 1976. I inhale deeply—the mossy stone walls, Queen Anne's lace, freshly cut grass—and something inside me rests in a way I never am able to in California. The West Coast is larger than life: an epic landscape that bowls you over with its grandeur. Maine's beauty is more personal. You can grab hold of it.

Sara slides Josie into an ExerSaucer.

"Do you think it's okay that I put her in there? This thing is a lifesaver. I never used it with the boys."

"How could it not be okay? Look at how happy she is," I say. Josie shrieks with delight and begins bouncing away. "Plus she's working off that baby fat."

My tiny sister gave birth to a baby that weighed nearly ten pounds. Josie still has rolls of fat around her ankles, her knees and the back of her neck. It's a very charming look. Provided you are nine months old.

"We had an ExerSaucer, a baby swing and a jumper for Ben," I say.

"A jumper?" says Sara. "Aren't they dangerous?"

I shrug. "Ben turned out okay, other than bouncing on his toes when he eats or takes a spelling test."

We have a long, leisurely dinner. The boys play in the yard. We have a second and then a third round of beers. And then we remember Josie, who is still in the saucer.

"Oh my God, she's been in there so long," says Sara.

Sara's husband lifts her out and when he does he finds she's had a little accident. Okay, a big accident. Not only is *she* covered in poop, but so are the fabric sling and the ExerSaucer. I would like to be the kind of aunt for whom an explosive bowel movement is not a big deal, but unfortunately I'm not. They aren't going to ask me to help, are they? I get up quickly and begin clearing the table, while Sara and her husband negotiate the triage.

"I'll give her a bath, you clean the saucer," says her husband.

Clearly Sara's stuck with the more disgusting job, but she goes at it like a pro. She unsnaps the sling, folds it in thirds and disappears into the laundry room. A few minutes later Sara's husband comes downstairs with Josie wrapped in a hooded towel.

"Sweet girl," I croon. "Are you all cleaned up?"

She babbles at me, and Sara's husband beams.

"Isn't she gorgeous?" he asks.

"She is. She's the most beautiful baby," I say.

Sara comes back from the laundry room and makes a beeline for Josie, kissing her on the cheek. Her face sours.

"Did you give her a bath?" she says.

"Yes, of course I gave her a bath," says her husband. "Can't you see she's all wet? She's dripping."

"Did you wash her hair?"

"Sure, I washed her hair."

"With shampoo?"

"She didn't need shampoo. She didn't shit on her head."

Sara takes a sniff of Josie. "Did you wash her body?"

"Yes, I washed her body."

"With soap?"

"Well, no. With water. I got all the poop off, though. That's what's important."

"You didn't use soap?"

"It's okay. You're not supposed to always use soap. It dries out their skin. Water is much better. Hey, I don't always use soap. Lots of times I take a shower and just use water," he says.

"Oh, my God," I say. "Thank you. You've made this so easy. Now I know what to get you for Christmas this year. Now I know what I'll get you for Christmas every year."

"We don't celebrate Christmas. We only *host* Christmas," says her husband. "Men don't like soft soap. Men like bar soap. Irish Spring. If there was some Irish Spring around here I'd use it."

"Take Josie back upstairs and give her another bath. WITH SOAP," says Sara.

"I'd appreciate it if you didn't tell your mother about this," says Sara's husband to me.

I spy Ben in the corner, gagging a little bit. That afternoon he'd asked if he could hold Josie. He was a good older cousin. He held her and sang to her and brought her toys. But when she spit up he panicked and tossed her to me as if she were a doll. He's a typical only child, not used to messes, fighting, or baths without soap.

"It's only poop," I say.

He covers his mouth and gags a little more.

The next morning when I wake, I can't open my left eye. I stagger downstairs, clutching the rail.

"There's something wrong with my eye," I tell Sara.

"Let me see."

I take off my glasses and she looks at it. "It doesn't really look swollen. Just a little red. It's probably a stye. Try a warm compress," she says, handing me a washcloth.

I sit at the breakfast table, holding the washcloth to my eye. Sara brings me coffee and a waffle. Every now and then I yell, "Ow," as my eye throbs with a piercing pain. Sara is compassionate at first but then gets a little annoyed.

"You know, I haven't had a stye for years, but I don't remember them being that painful. Maybe you should go back to bed? Do you think you could stop saying *ow*? You're frightening the kids."

I am trying to be a good trooper, but then I get a little annoyed.

"This doesn't feel like a stye. I would go back to bed, but I'm enjoying Julian's kicking my ankle under the table so much that why would I leave?"

I go to the ophthalmologist's. He's a warm fellow with a wonderful bedside manner.

"What happened? Did you get drunk and fall on your eye?" he asks.

"Please, can you just give me some eyedrops?" I beg him. "The numbing kind."

"Well, look at that," he said, shining a light in my eye. "You've scratched your cornea. Did you walk into a tree branch? You probably don't remember because you were so drunk."

"I didn't do anything. My eyes hurt last night so I took out my contacts and put on my glasses. I woke up like this."

"Uh-huh," he says.

"So what happens now? You give me some eyedrops?"

He wheels away from me in his chair. "You are one step away from a corneal ulcer," he says.

"An ulcer? Is that serious?"

"People with ulcers need corneal transplants. So, yes, it's serious."

"You're kidding?"

"I am not kidding."

"Are you trying to scare me?"

"You bet," he says. "No contacts for a month. You'll have to wear your glasses. Hopefully you haven't done any permanent damage, but we won't know for a while. Maybe next time you'll think twice about having that third margarita and going for a walk in the woods."

He cracks a smile.

"I'm worried," I say. "You're really worrying me."

"You should be worried," he says, handing me an eye patch.

"That eye will be extremely sensitive to light. I'm writing out a prescription for some eyedrops. You may use them three times a day. No more than that or it will slow down the healing. Do you understand?"

"Is it an anesthetic?" I say. "Will it stop the pain?"

"Yes, but use it no more than three times a day."

See, I am not a big fat baby," I say to Sara when I get back to the house. "I am one step away from a corneal ulcer."

She gasps, but it comes out like a snort because she's also trying not to laugh. I'm wearing my eye patch, with my glasses over the eye patch and my sunglasses over the eye patch and the glasses. Julian and Alek cling to Sara's legs like they have no idea who I am.

"The light. It hurts. It feels like somebody is sticking a toothpick in my eye."

"Can you drive?" Sara asks. Tomorrow Ben and I are supposed to depart for mid-coast Maine. "There's always the bus," she says.

"We're not taking the bus. I'm sure I'll feel better tomorrow. The doctor said no contacts for a month. Damn. I hate wearing my glasses!"

Julian looks up at me, his little blue glasses cloudy with fingerprint smudges, charmingly askew on his face.

"Because they aren't blue. If they were blue I'd love them. If only they made blue glasses for grown-ups."

I do hate wearing my glasses. I haven't worn them full-time since I was a girl. My glasses period was traumatizing. If I wasn't losing them and getting grounded for losing them, or falling on top of them and crushing them, I was making very bad choices in the optometrist's office. I had John Denver glasses when I was seven. I had gigantic pink frames when I was in middle school.

My vision was so bad that without glasses I had to be two or three inches away from a mirror to see my face and at that distance everything was distorted. It wasn't until I got contacts at fifteen that I was finally able to see what I really looked like. It was a shock. I have been wearing contacts every day, twelve hours a day, for twenty-eight years. When I put on my glasses now I feel disoriented. Lost.

"I'm not faking it. It really hurts," I say to Sara, fighting off tears.

"Oh, Mel," she says. "Let's get you to bed."

She puts me down for a nap with the rest of the kids and between the hours of one and three the entire household sleeps. *The way life should be*—this is Maine's motto—and it's true, barring corneal scratches.

It's a foolish thing to do, but the next morning I drive to mid-coast Maine. I've completely disregarded the doctor's instructions and I've been putting in the eyedrops almost hourly and they haven't helped a bit. I'm beginning to suspect the doctor gave me a placebo. Weaving down the highway, praying for clouds, wearing my patch and glasses and sunglasses—I feel like an old lady pirate.

"Watch out for that guy selling blueberries!" says Ben.

He's had to say this at least five times already. There're an awful lot of people selling blueberries heading north on Route 1.

I swerve to the left. My depth perception is nil.

"Just keep your eyes on the road. Let me know if I'm getting too close to the embankment," I tell him. "That's your job."

Finally, nearly two hours later, we arrive and I step out of the driver's seat, exhausted. I want nothing more than to crawl back into bed. This is the first year we've rented a house—normally we stay with my mother-in-law—and it's always a bit of Russian roulette when you rent a place sight unseen. I cross my fingers and unlock the door of our rental. As soon as we step over the threshold we both groan with happiness. Ben actually begins jumping up and down. It's the kind of house you feel like you've been waiting for all your life. You knew it existed, but you just didn't know how to get there.

The house is called Owl's Ledge. It's got floor-to-ceiling windows and is filled with light and through every window you get the same stunning view: a green bowl of a meadow that leads straight down to the sea. Best of all is my bedroom. There is nothing in it but a bed. A bed that gives instructions, that issues a mandate. There are three things you can do in this room: nap, read, and well, you can guess the third.

A rhythm is quickly established. We sleep late. We wander down to the ocean, me with a mug of coffee, Ben with a butterfly net. We spend a couple of hours sitting on the rocks and poking around. There's so much to see and smell and absorb. The leaves of the birch trees make a sound like gold coins pouring from a hand. The air smells of hay, sunscreen and pine needles. I'm like Frederick the mouse in that Leo Lionni book, gathering sun, colors and words for the rest of the year when we're living three thousand miles away from this beloved place where both my son and Bodhi were born.

When Ben gets bored, he wanders down the shore to my mother-in-law's house and they go off to the dump, to the bakery or to Cod End for fried clams and I go back to the house, crawl into my bed and sleep some more.

I give up on the eyedrops. The only cure for a scratched cornea is time. I try and have faith that this is all happening for a reason. My sight needed to be reassembled.

Wearing my glasses, I feel I'm under a spell. Time has reversed itself and I'm a girl again. When I lived in absolutes. When I knew exactly what I loved and what I hated. When pain was not a stranger but a familiar visitor. Some part of my body was always bleeding or skinned, because I was always falling, because I was always risking something. Pain with a beginning and an end. Pain that could be ridden out.

They call that innocence.

I think about Ben. And how the veil of his innocence is being lifted. About the things he used to know. And what he'll forget. And what, one day, if he's lucky, he'll remember again. When he was three he told me grapes tasted like sadness. When he was four he told his father I was king of all the womens. When he was seven he told his best friend he didn't need to go to heaven because he was already living inside of God.

I am so relieved when my husband comes.

"Give me the car keys," is the first thing he says.

I hand them over.

"You are now officially relieved of your chauffeuring duties."

I don't tell him we've barely left Owl's Ledge since we've gotten here and he won't want to either.

The time away from each other has been good. It was time enough to really miss him, and as the days pass, I begin to recognize him again. This is what happens when you've been together for nearly twenty years. You become strangers and then you recognize each other and then you become strangers again and you repeat this pattern—this loop, this skein—over and over again.

I watch him in his competence steering a Boston Whaler up the St. George River at low tide in the fog, teaching our son how to paddle a kayak and ferrying his half-blind wife around the Port Clyde peninsula. We swim in lakes. We read the entire Sunday *New York Times*. We are happy.

And finally it's our last night before we leave Maine. We're at my mother-in-law's house and a large group of cousins and aunts and uncles have gathered—all from my husband's side of the family. We've eaten dinner and we've made our way through numerous bottles of wine. We have been talking about everything except why we are gathered here.

Why we are gathered here is the reason my son is on a couch crying softly. Tonight we are burying Bodhi. Ben's holding the gallon-size Ziploc baggie on his lap. Every now and then he shakes the bag, his version of petting the dog.

We have chosen a special place in my mother-in-law's garden where Bodhi's ashes will go, between the lemon mint and the pachysandra. There is a stone angel marking the spot, but as we get closer to actually putting him there and saying our last words, Ben gets more and more visibly upset.

Finally I kneel down and whisper to Ben, "We don't have to leave him here."

"We don't?" asks Ben.

"No," I say. "I don't think it's the right thing. I did, but I don't anymore. I thought because he was born here we should bury him here. But he needs to be where we are. That's where he belongs. With us. We'll take him back."

"Home?" Ben asks me.

"Yes, home," I say.

Home—the ways in which we are bound to one another. Not by chance. Not by country or house or blood, but by choice. I see now that home has always been *my choice*. We leave the door open. Or we seal it shut. We run away. Or we choose to stay.

Sometimes the days burst open like seedpods and we see thousands of futures, and it's so much that our throats swell and we can't do anything but turn away and try and forget that gleaming, all that possibility. Who could live into such brightness? Sometimes the days beat their wings slowly so we can take their measure, so we know how lucky we are that we are being given just one moment more.

"We're going to get stopped by airport security again," I whisper to my husband. "You do realize that this particular incarnation of Bodhi bears a peculiar resemblance to a pound of coke?"

"Don't worry," says my husband. "I'll take care of it."

"Good sit," my son whispers to the Ziploc baggie when he thinks everybody has stopped listening.

Later we walk back to Owl's Ledge, picking our way along the shore: our small family—a mother, a father and a boy carrying his dog. We are enough. We are just as we should be. Our bellies are full with good food and good wine. Our clothes smell of wood smoke, and our hair smells of the sea. Tonight our son adores us. We haven't lost him yet, to his friends, to music, to love. Changes are ahead. Low tides. But right now we are walking beneath a starry sky, bathed in the moon's light.

Acknowledgments

I am deeply grateful to my agent, Elizabeth Sheinkman, for believing in this book, understanding it before I even had words for it, and for finding it such a good home. I can't say enough about Jordan Pavlin—sorcerer, midwife, and friend—in short, the editor of my dreams. Thanks also to the entire team at Knopf, most especially Leslie Levine, Sarah Gelman, and Paul Bogaards. Also thanks to Felicity Blunt and Betsy Robbins at Curtis-Brown UK.

A huge thank-you to all my friends and family for their generosity and counsel: Kerri Arsenault, Brigeda Bank, Laura Barnard, Natalie Baszile, Allison Bartlett, Elizabeth Bernstein, Kathleen Caldwell, Kathryn Fox, Helena Echlin, Carol Edgarian, Rodes Fishburne; my sisters, Dawn, Rebecca and Sara Gideon; my parents, Sarah and Vasant Gideon; Joanne Hartman, Robin Heller, Jeanne Martin, Alexandra Merrill, Caroline Paul, Elizabeth Pelzner,

Lisa Ruben, Beth Schoenberger, Renee Schoepflin, Cameron Tuttle, Ken Vivian, and, last but not at all least, my fellow writers at the Grotto.

Thank you to Charlotte Sheedy—one of the classiest women I know.

Thanks to Dan Jones, for publishing the Modern Love essay that was the seed for *The Slippery Year*.

And finally, abiding thanks to my husband and son for letting me tell our story.